RECORDED VERSIONS
GUITAR

**AUTHENTIC TRANSCRIPTIONS
WITH NOTES AND TABLATURE**

Ed Sheeran

X

ISBN 978-1-4950-0420-9

HAL•LEONARD®
CORPORATION

7777 W. BLUEMOUND RD. P.O. BOX 13819 MILWAUKEE, WI 53213

Visit Hal Leonard Online at
www.halleonard.com

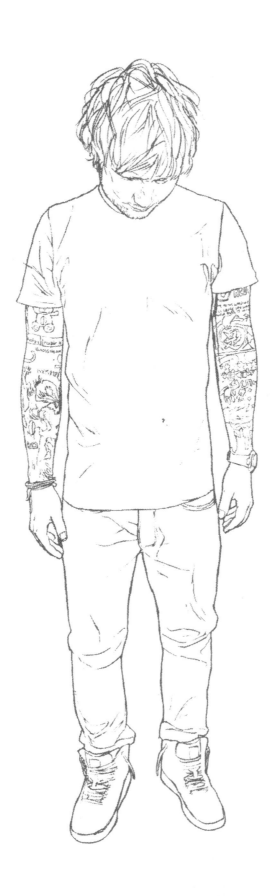

Guitar tablature explained

Guitar music can be explained in three different ways: on a musical stave, in tablature, and in rhythm slashes.

RHYTHM SLASHES: are written above the stave. Strum chords in the rhythm indicated. Round noteheads indicate single notes.

THE MUSICAL STAVE: shows pitches and rhythms and is divided by lines into bars. Pitches are named after the first seven letters of the alphabet.

TABLATURE: graphically represents the guitar fingerboard. Each horizontal line represents a string, and each number represents a fret.

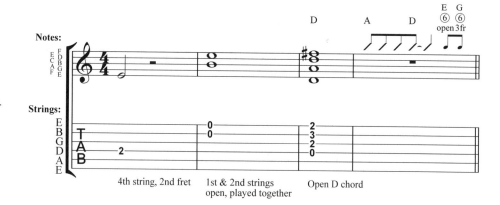

4th string, 2nd fret   1st & 2nd strings open, played together   Open D chord

Definitions for special guitar notation

SEMI-TONE BEND: Strike the note and bend up a semi-tone (½ step).

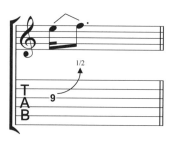

WHOLE-TONE BEND: Strike the note and bend up a whole-tone (full step).

GRACE NOTE BEND: Strike the note and bend as indicated. Play the first note as quickly as possible.

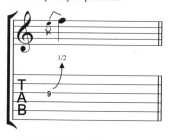

QUARTER-TONE BEND: Strike the note and bend up a ¼ step

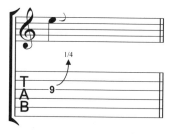

BEND & RELEASE: Strike the note and bend up as indicated, then release back to the original note.

COMPOUND BEND & RELEASE: Strike the note and bend up and down in the rhythm indicated.

PRE-BEND: Bend the note as indicated, then strike it.

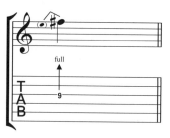

PRE-BEND & RELEASE: Bend the note as indicated. Strike it and release the note back to the original pitch.

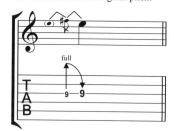

HAMMER-ON: Strike the first note with one finger, then sound the second note (on the same string) with another finger by fretting it without picking.

PULL-OFF: Place both fingers on the note to be sounded, strike the first note and without picking, pull the finger off to sound the second note.

LEGATO SLIDE (GLISS): Strike the first note and then slide the same fret-hand finger up or down to the second note. The second note is not struck.

MUFFLED STRINGS: A percussive sound is produced by laying the first hand across the string(s) without depressing, and striking them with the pick hand.

NATURAL HARMONIC: Strike the note while the fret-hand lightly touches the string directly over the fret indicated.

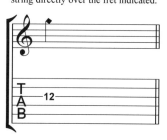

PICK SCRAPE: The edge of the pick is rubbed down (or up) the string, producing a scratchy sound.

PALM MUTING: The note is partially muted by the pick hand lightly touching the string(s) just before the bridge.

SHIFT SLIDE (GLISS & RESTRIKE) Same as legato slide, except the second note is struck.

TAP HARMONIC: The note is fretted normally and a harmonic is produced by tapping or slapping the fret indicated in brackets (which will be twelve frets higher than the fretted note.)

TAPPING: Hammer ('tap') the fret indicated with the pick-hand index or middle finger and pull-off to the note fretted by the fret hand.

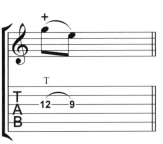

PINCH HARMONIC: The note is fretted normally and a harmonic is produced by adding the edge of the thumb or the tip of the index finger of the pick hand to the normal pick attack.

ARTIFICIAL HARMONIC: The note fretted normally and a harmonic is produced by gently resting the pick hand's index finger directly above the indicated fret (in brackets) while plucking the appropriate string.

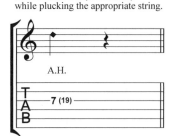

TRILL: Very rapidly alternate between the notes indicated by continuously hammering-on and pulling-off.

RAKE: Drag the pick across the strings with a single motion.

TREMOLO PICKING: The note is picked as rapidly and continuously as possible.

ARPEGGIATE: Play the notes of the chord indicated by quickly rolling them from bottom to top.

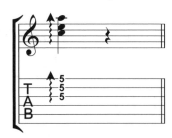

SWEEP PICKING: Rhythmic downstroke and/or upstroke motion across the strings.

VIBRATO DIVE BAR AND RETURN: The pitch of the note or chord is dropped a specific number of steps (in rhythm) then returned to the original pitch.

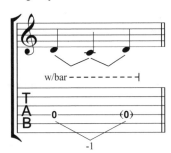

VIBRATO BAR SCOOP: Depress the bar just before striking the note, then quickly release the bar.

VIBRATO BAR DIP: Strike the note and then immediately drop a specific number of steps, then release back to the original pitch.

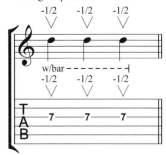

Additional musical definitions

 (accent) Accentuate note (play it louder)

D.S. al Coda Go back to the sign (𝄋), then play until the bar marked *To Coda* ⊕ then skip to the section marked ⊕ *Coda*

 (accent) Accentuate note with greater intensity

D.C. al Fine Go back to the beginning of the song and play until the bar marked *Fine.*

 (staccato) Shorten time value of note

tacet Instrument is silent (drops out).

⊓ Downstroke

∨ Upstroke

Repeat bars between signs

NOTE: Tablature numbers in brackets mean:
1. The note is sustained, but a new articulation (such as hammer-on or slide) begins
2. A note may be fretted but not necessarily played.

1. | 2.

When a repeat section has different endings, play the first ending only the first time and the second ending only the second time.

5

One

Words and Music by Ed Sheeran

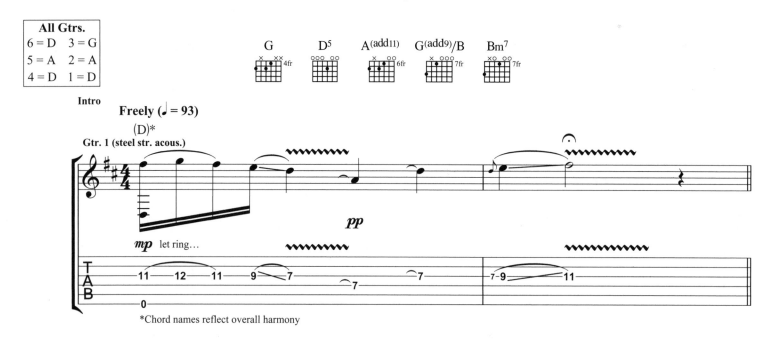

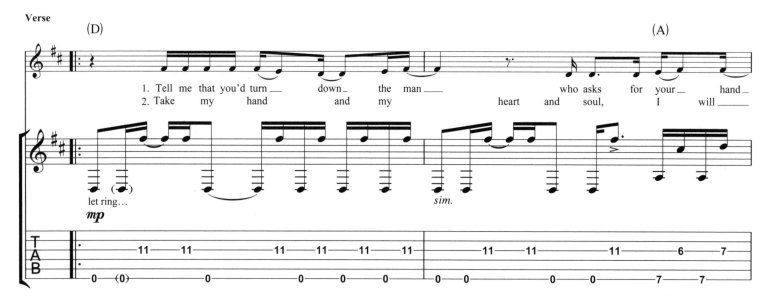

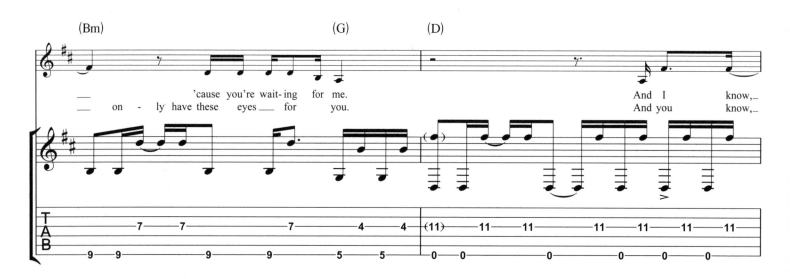

I am so gone, so tell me the way home.

I listen to sad songs, singing about love,

and where it goes wrong.

Ooh.

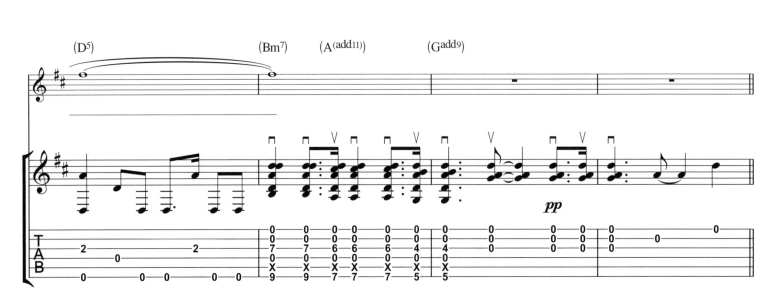

Outro Chorus

All my sen - ses come to life ___ while I'm stum - bling home as

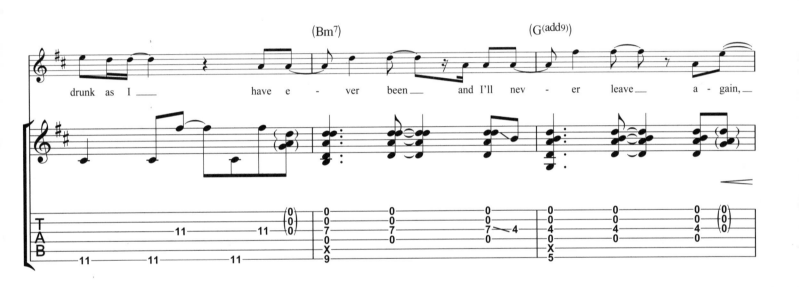

drunk as I ___ have e - ver been ___ and I'll nev - er leave ___ a - gain, ___

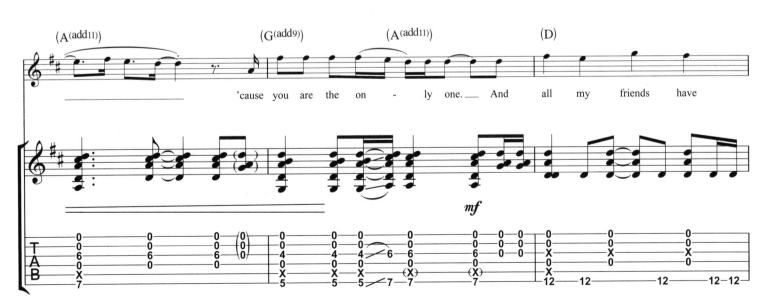

'cause you are the on - ly one. ___ And all my friends have

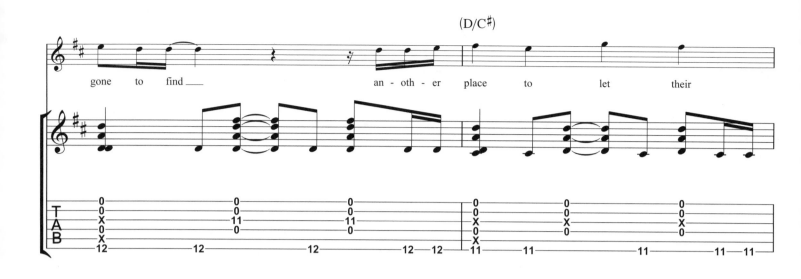

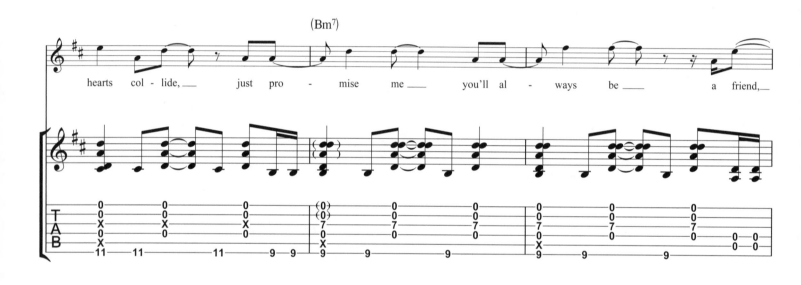

12

I'm a Mess

Words and Music by Ed Sheeran

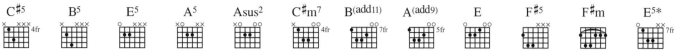

To match original recording, tune all guitars down a semitone

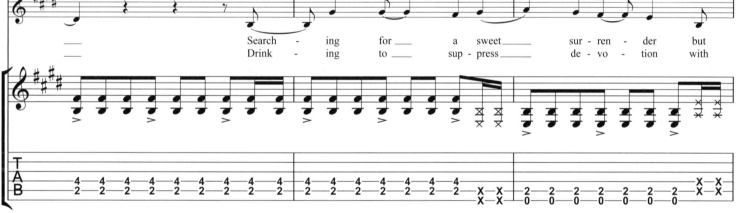

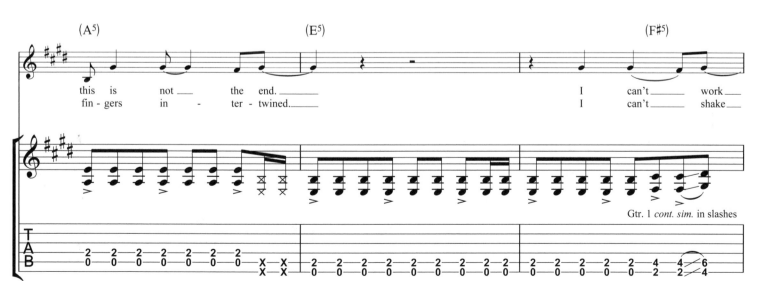

Sing

Words and Music by Ed Sheeran and Pharrell Williams

To match original recording, tune all guitars down a semitone

Lyrics:
1. It's late in the evening, glass on the side, I've been sat with you for most of the night. Ignoring ev'rybody here, we wish they would disappear so maybe we could get down now. I don't wanna know

if you're get-ting a-head___ of the pro-gram, I want you to ___ be mine,___

Dm⁷

la-dy,___ and to hold your bo-dy close,___ take a-no-ther step in-to the no ___

___ man's land, for the long-est time,___ la-dy. ___ I

Chorus

(Am)

need you dar-ling, come on set the tone,___ if you

Gtr. 1

w/percussive feel
Gtrs. 3+4 tacet

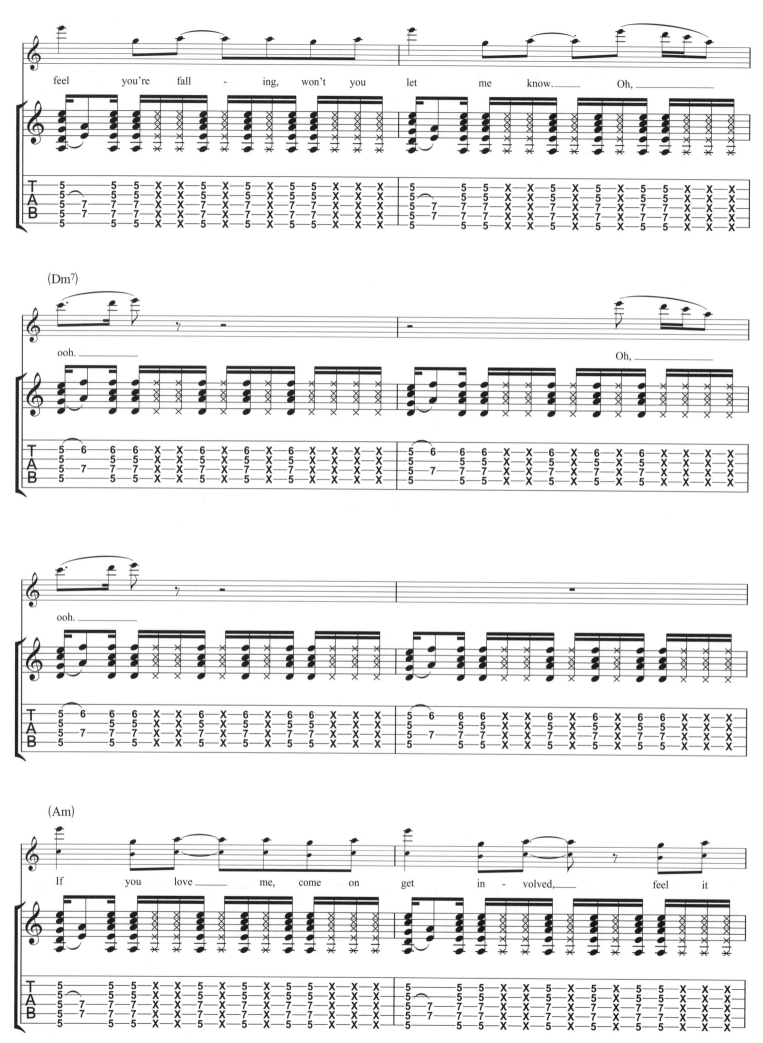

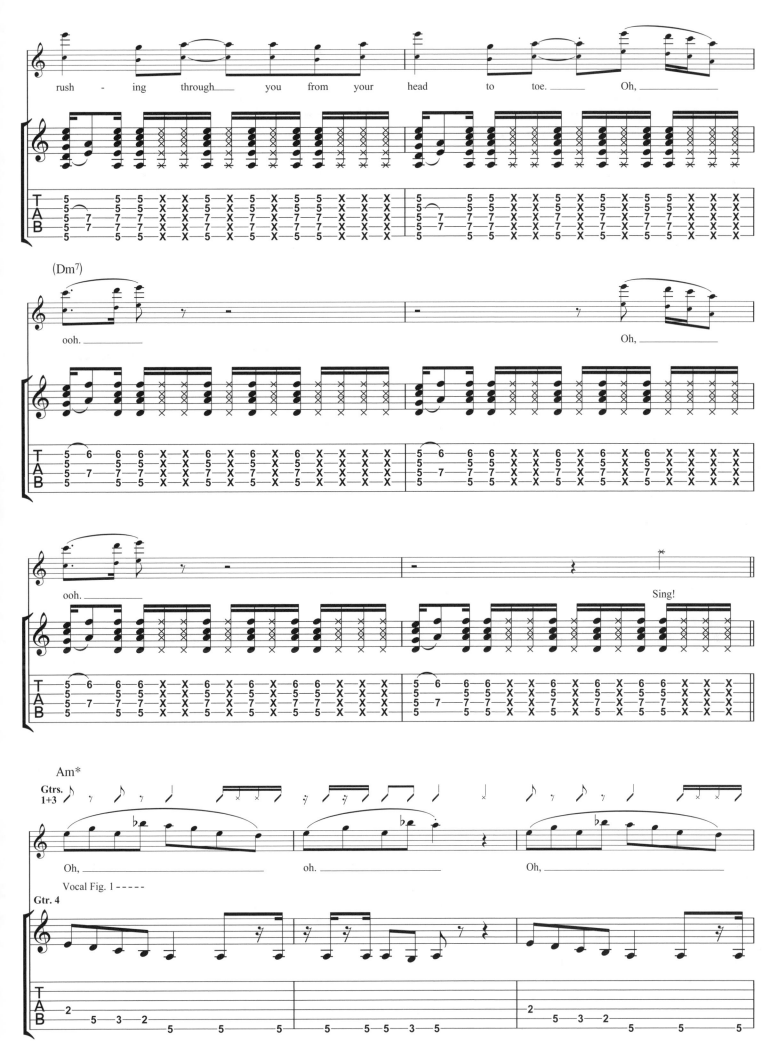

deep___ if an-y-bo-dy finds out, I'm meant___ to drive home but I've drunk all of it now. Not

D.S. al Coda

so-ber-ing up we just sit on the couch,___ one thing___ led to an-oth-er now she's kiss-ing my mouth.___ I

⊕ *Coda*

Dm⁷   Gtrs. 1+2   Am

oh. _____   Can you feel _____ it? All the guys in here don't

Gtrs. 3+4 tacet

Dm⁷

ev-en wan-na dance.___ Can you feel _____ it? All that I can hear is

Don't

Words and Music by Ed Sheeran, Dawn Robinson, Ben Levin, Raphael Saadiq, Ali Jones-Muhammad and Conesha Owens

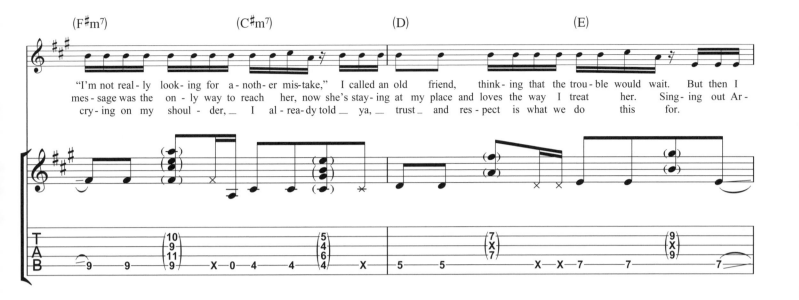

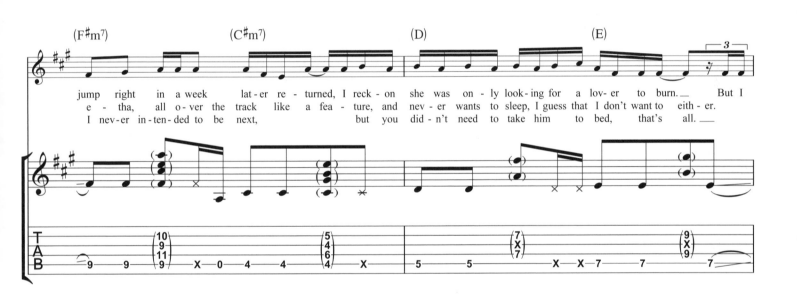

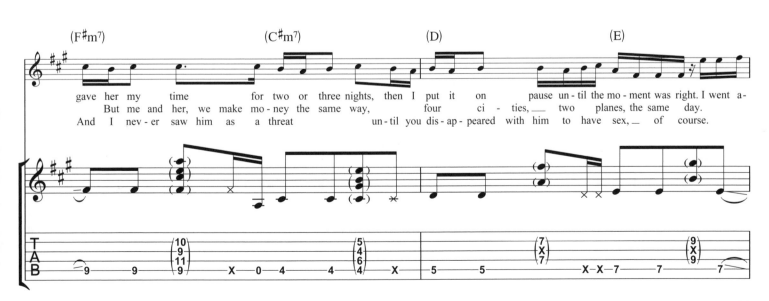

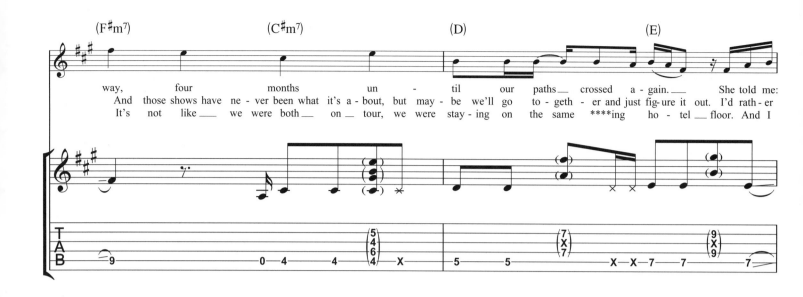

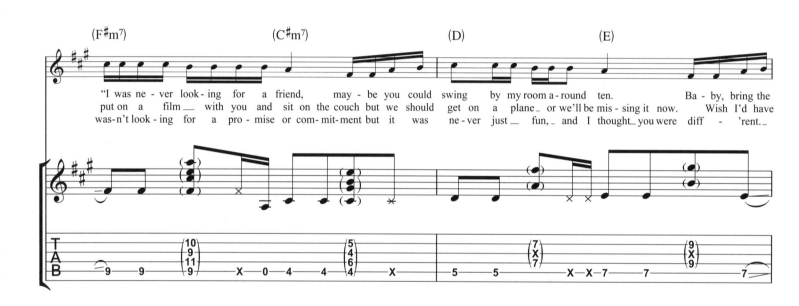

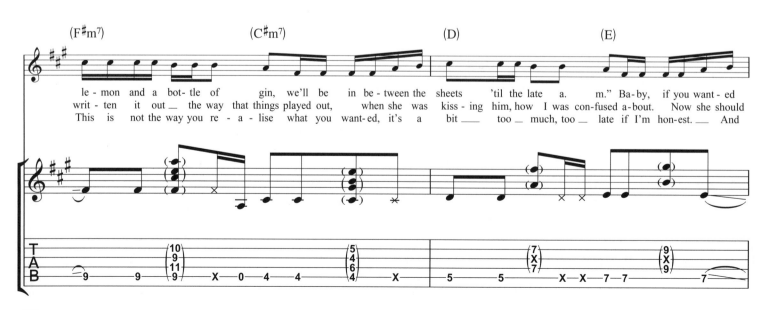

Nina

Words and Music by Ed Sheeran, Jermaine Scott, Isra Andja-Diumi Lohata, John McDaid and Jay Lee Robert Hippolyte

Photograph

Words and Music by Ed Sheeran and John McDaid

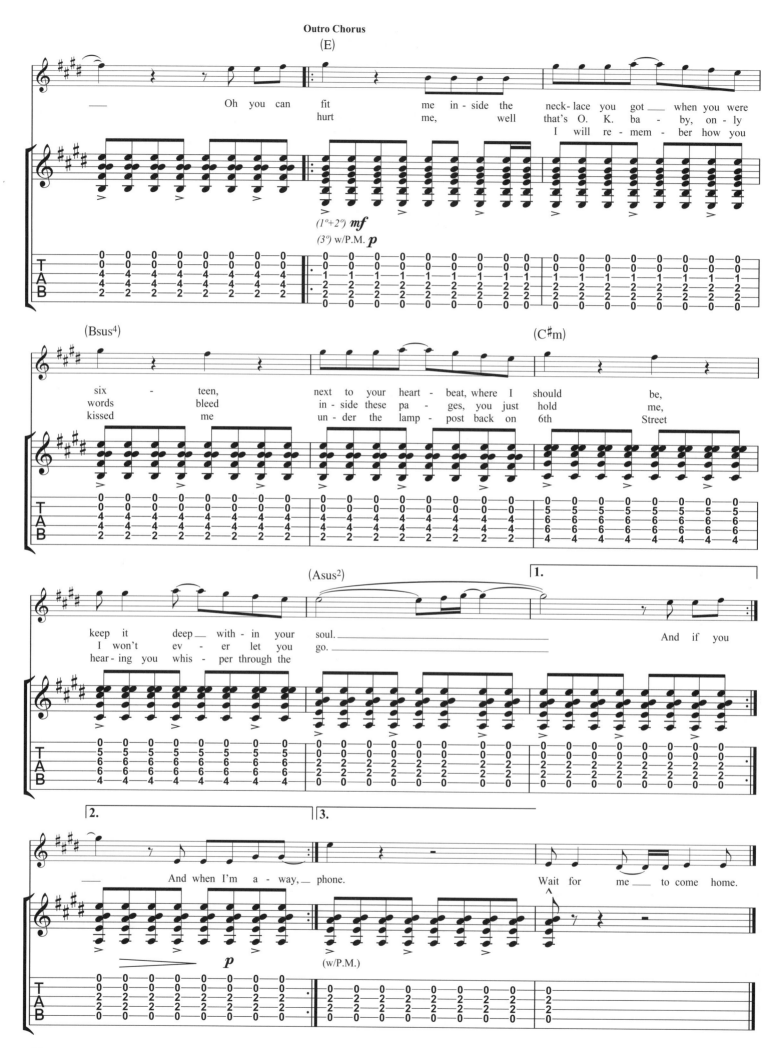

Bloodstream

Words and Music by Ed Sheeran, Amir Izadkhah, Kesi Dryden, Piers Aggett, John McDaid and Gary Lightbody

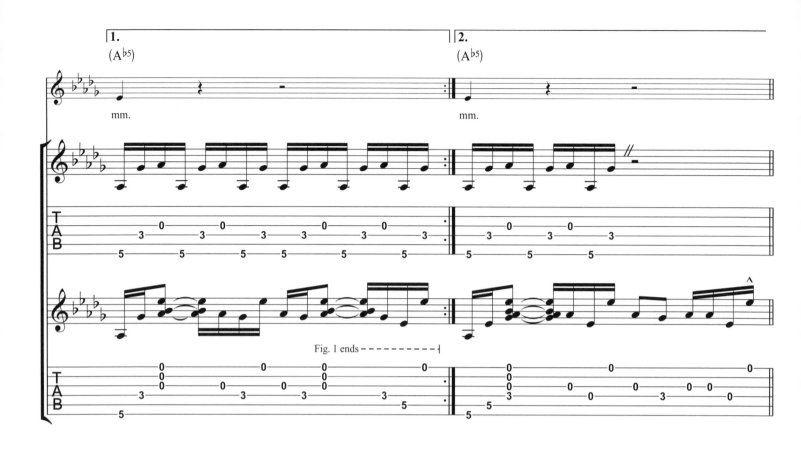

Verse

1. I've been spin-ning out of ___ time,   cou - ple wo-men by my ___ side,
2. I've been look-ing for a ___ lover,   thought I'd find her in a bott-le,

Gtr. 1

Gtr. 2 tacet

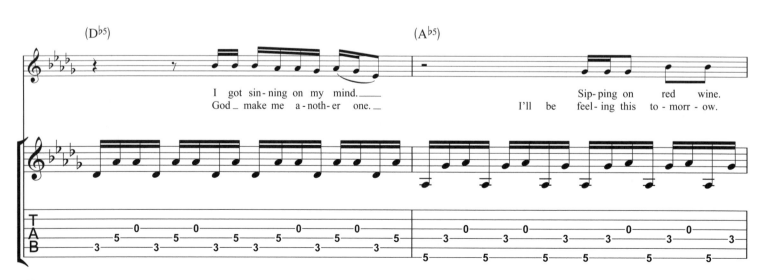

I got sin-ning on my mind.___   Sip-ping on   red wine.
God ___ make me a-noth-er one. ___   I'll be   feel-ing this to - morr - ow.

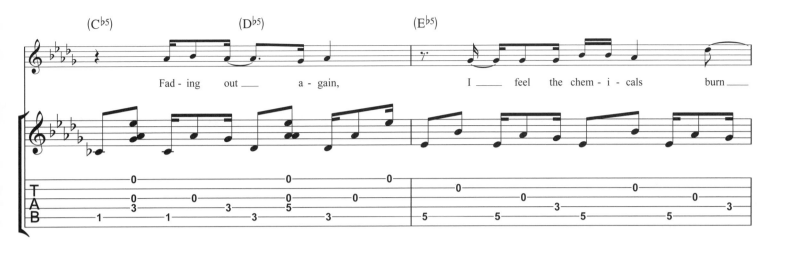

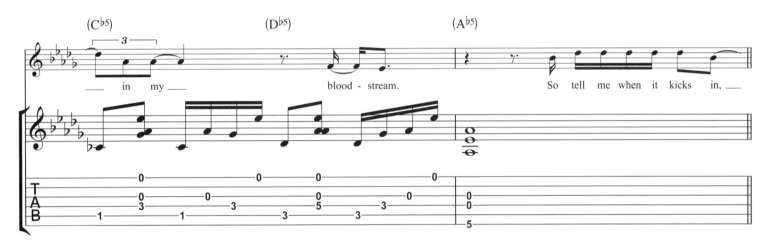

Chorus

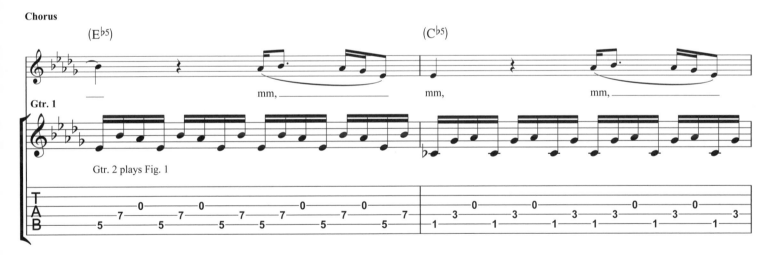

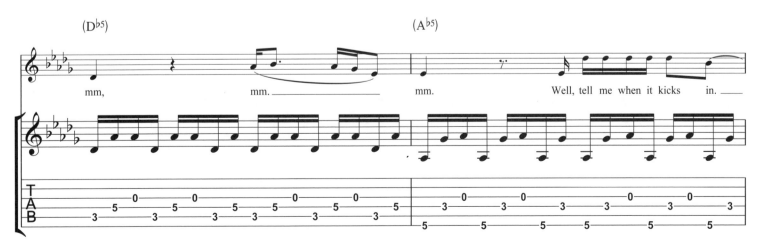

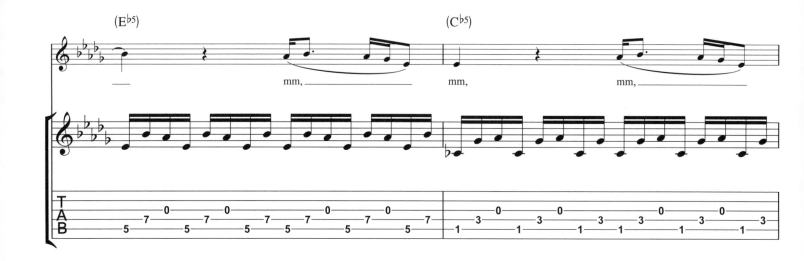

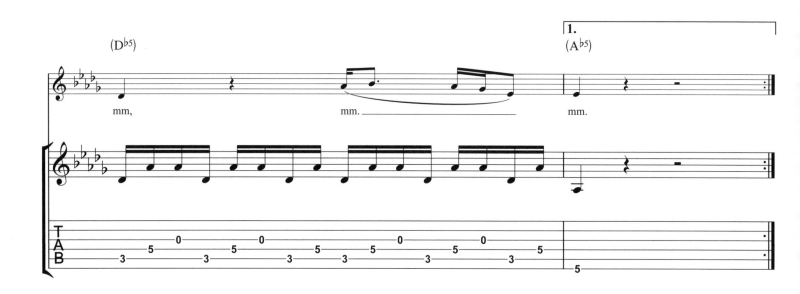

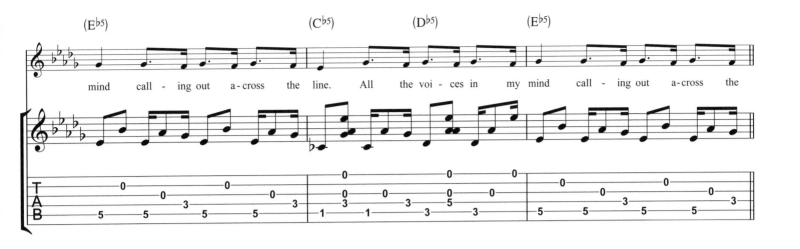

mind call - ing out a-cross the line. All the voi-ces in my mind call - ing out a-cross the

line. All the voi - ces in my mind call - ing out a - cross the

Vocal Fig. 1

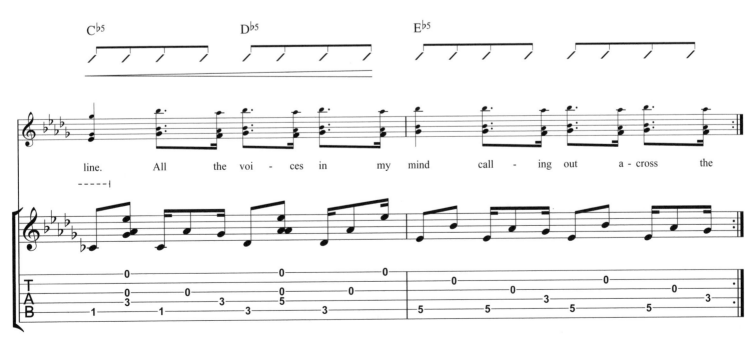

line. All the voi - ces in my mind call - ing out a - cross the

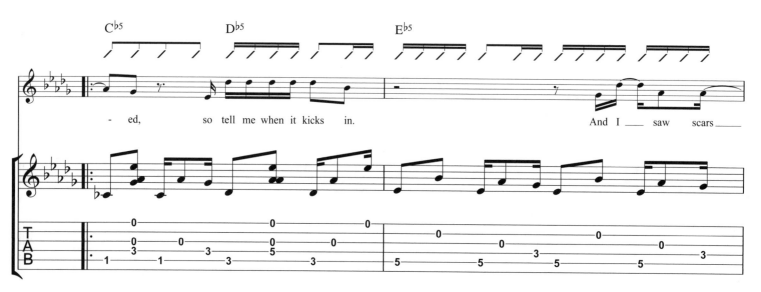

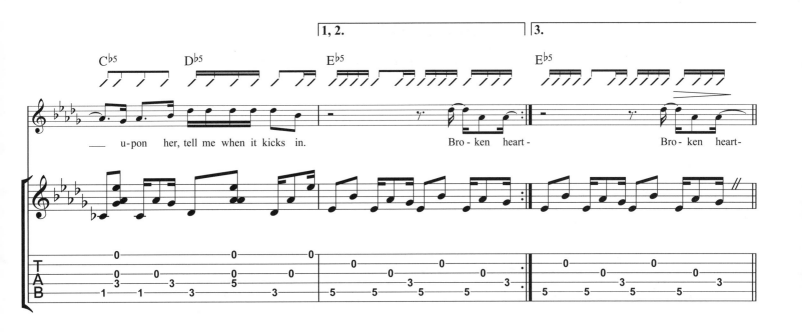

u-pon her, tell me when it kicks in.

Bro - ken heart -

Bro - ken heart-

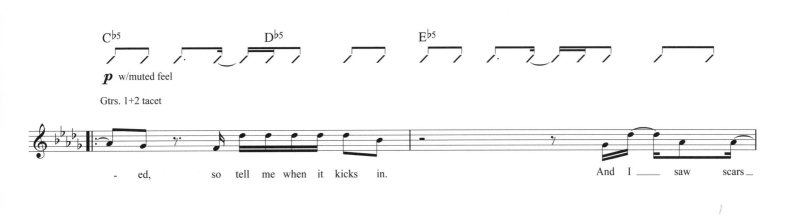

p w/muted feel

Gtrs. 1+2 tacet

- ed,   so tell me when it kicks in.

And I ___ saw scars ___

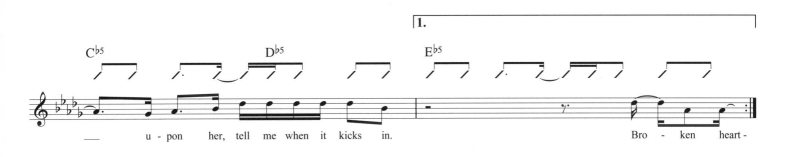

___   u - pon   her, tell me when it kicks in.

Bro - ken heart -

Bro - ken heart - ed,

Tenerife Sea

Words and Music by Ed Sheeran, John McDaid and Foy Vance

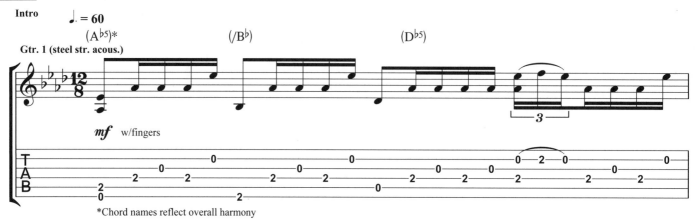

*Chord names reflect overall harmony

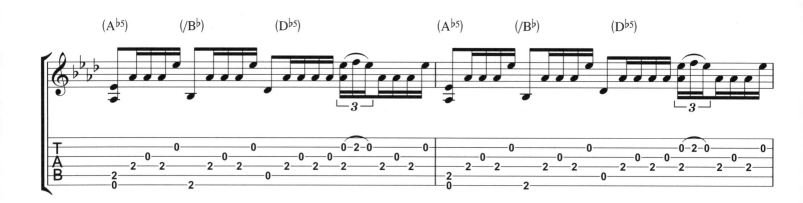

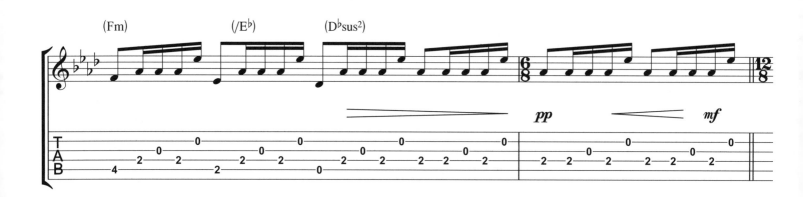

Verse

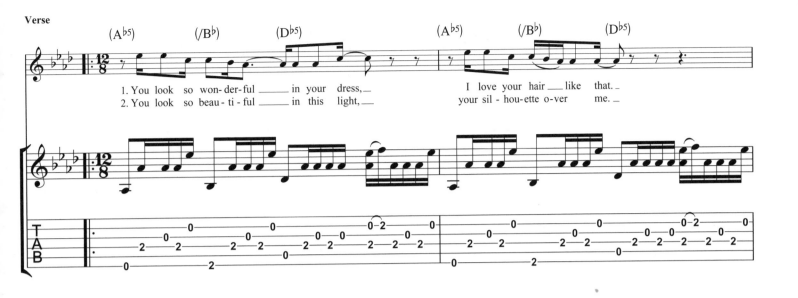

1. You look so won-der-ful ___ in your dress, ___ I love your hair ___ like that. ___
2. You look so beau-ti-ful ___ in this light, ___ your sil - hou-ette o-ver me. ___

The way it falls ___ on the side ___ of your ___ neck, ___ down your shoul-ders and back.
The way it brings ___ out the blue ___ in your eyes ___ is the Ten-er-ife Sea.

And

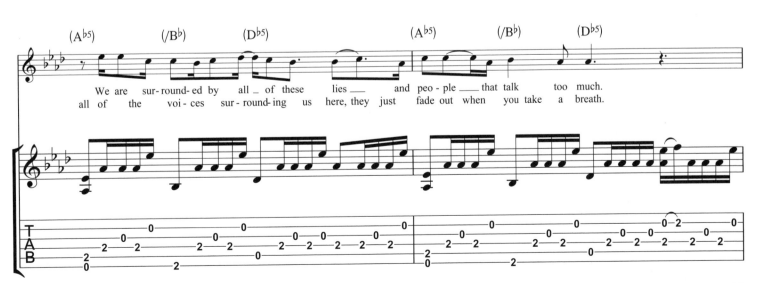

We are sur-round-ed by all ___ of these lies ___ and peo-ple ___ that talk too much.
all of the voi-ces sur-round-ing us here, they just fade out when you take a breath.

You got the kind _ of look _ in your eyes _ as if no _ one knows an-y-thing _ but us. _
Just say the word and now we'll dis-ap-pear in-to the wil - der-ness. _

Pre-chorus

Should this be _ the last _ thing I see, I want you to know _ that it's not for me. _ 'Cause

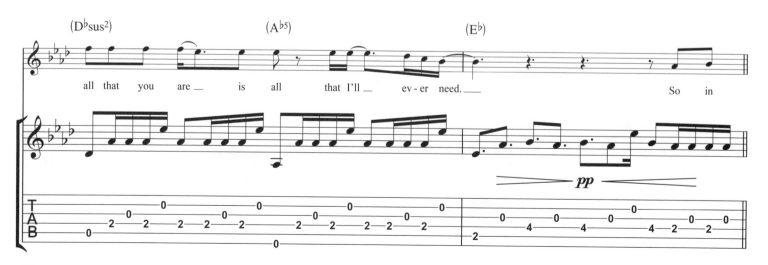

all that you are _ is all that I'll _ ev-er need. _ So in

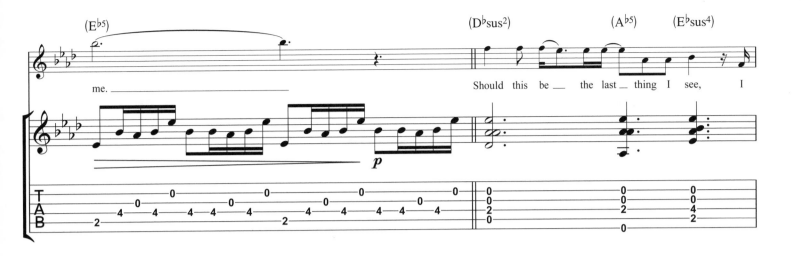

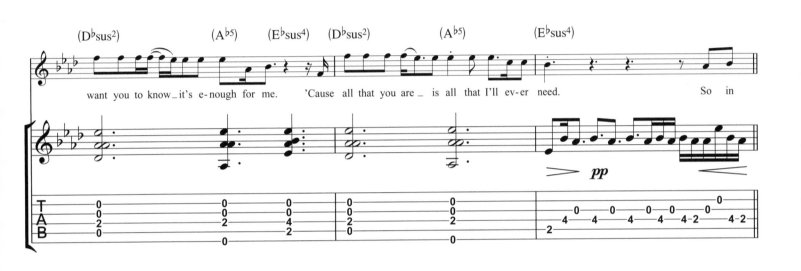

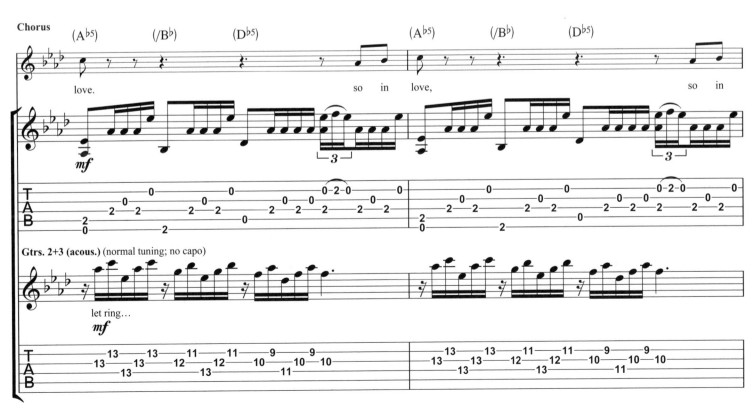

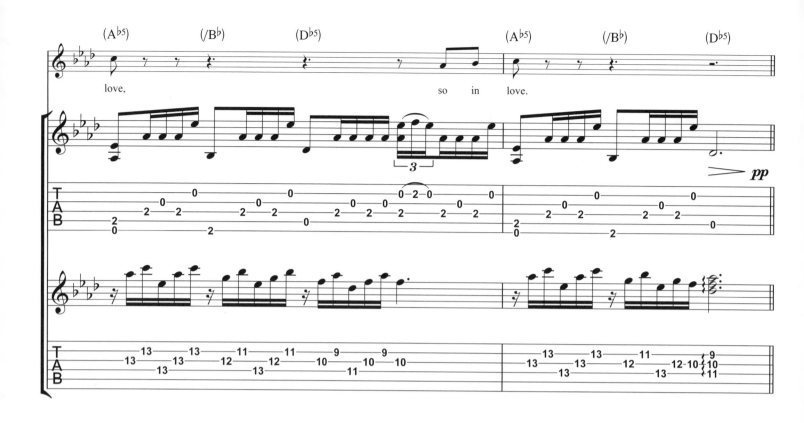

love, so in love.

Outro

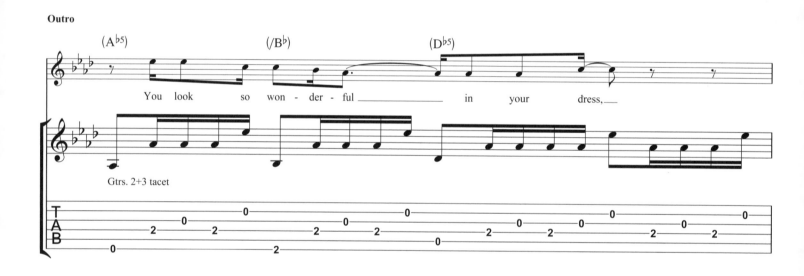

You look so won-der-ful _____ in your dress,____

Gtrs. 2+3 tacet

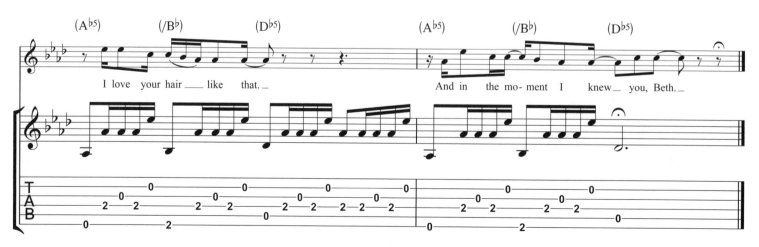

I love your hair ____ like that. ____ And in the mo-ment I knew___ you, Beth.____

Runaway

Words and Music by Ed Sheeran and Pharrell Williams

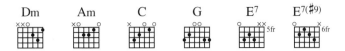

To match original recording, tune all guitars down a semitone

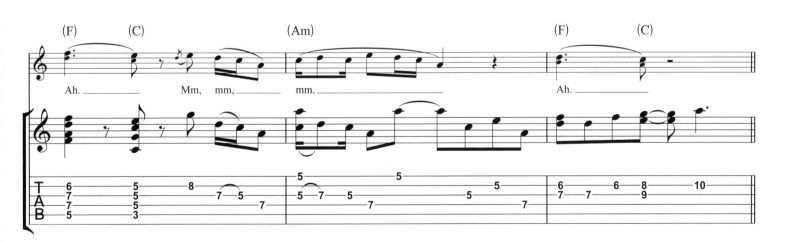

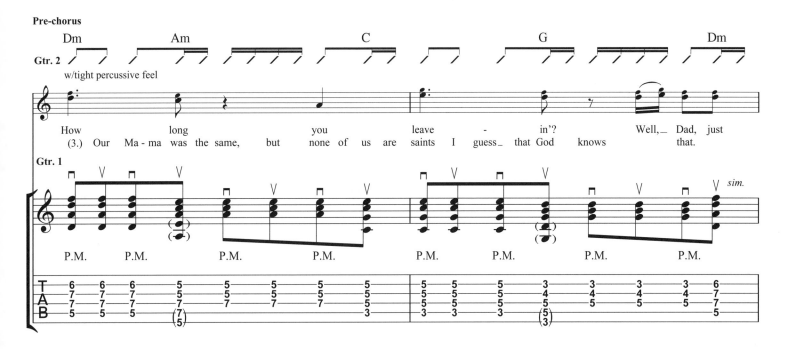

Pre-chorus

How long you leave - in'? Well,__ Dad, just
(3.) Our Ma - ma was the same, but none of us are saints I guess__ that God knows that.

P.M. P.M. P.M. P.M. P.M. P.M. P.M. P.M.

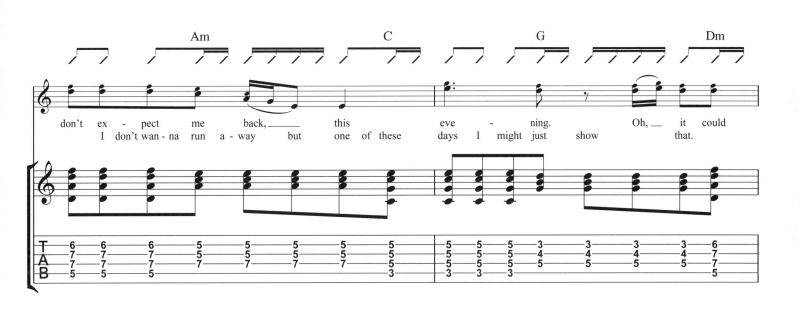

don't ex - pect me back,_____ this eve - ning. Oh,__ it could
I don't wan - na run a - way but one of these days I might just show that.

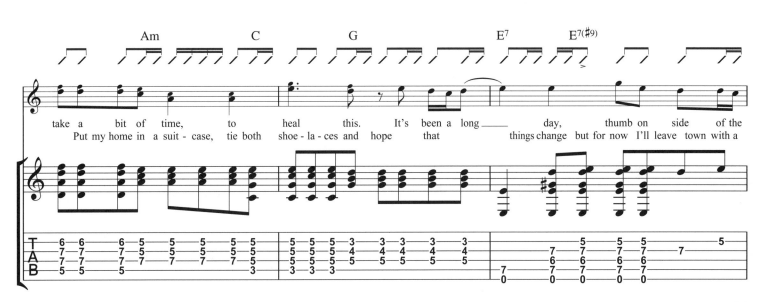

take a bit of time, to heal this. It's been a long _____ day, thumb on side of the
Put my home in a suit - case, tie both shoe - la - ces and hope that things change but for now I'll leave town with a

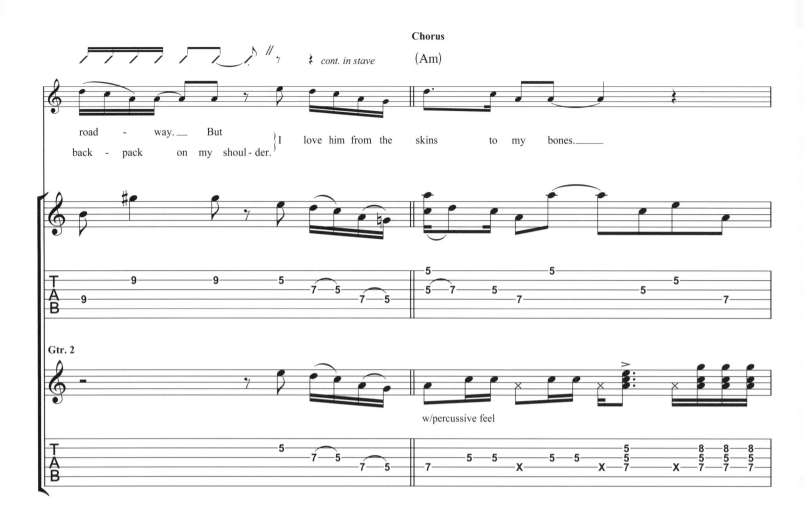

road - way.___ But { I love him from the skins to my bones.____

back - pack on my shoul - der. }

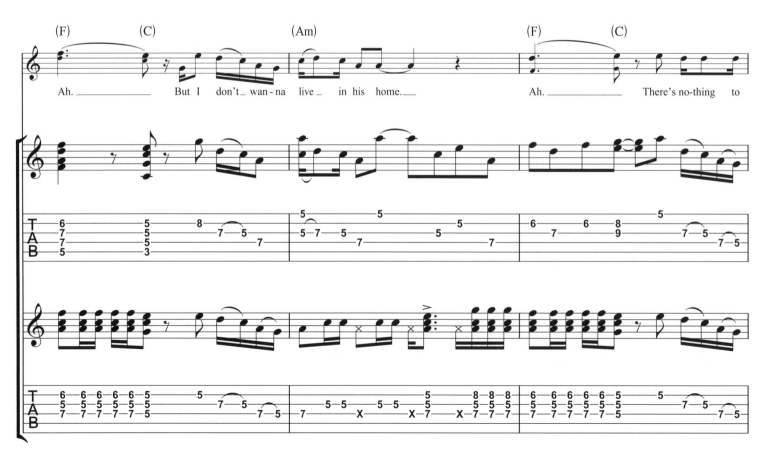

Ah. _____ But I don't_ wan - na live_ in his home.___ Ah. _____ There's no-thing to

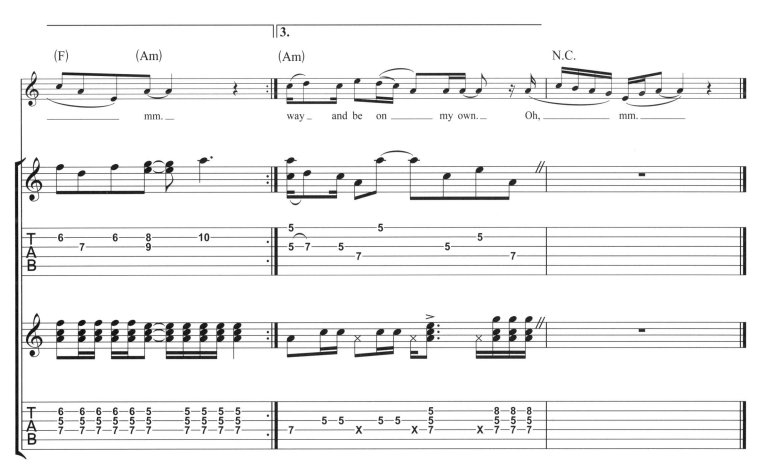

The Man

Words and Music by Ed Sheeran

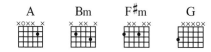

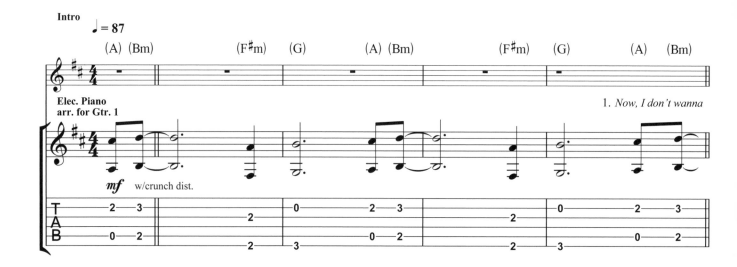

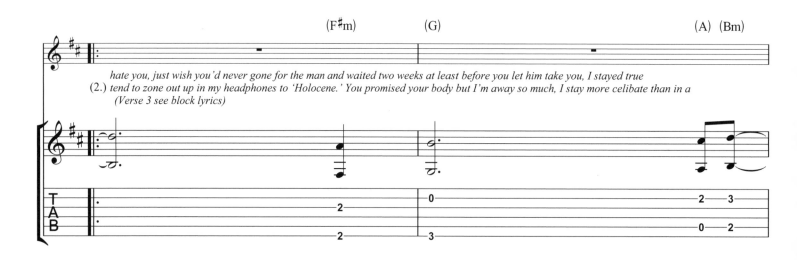

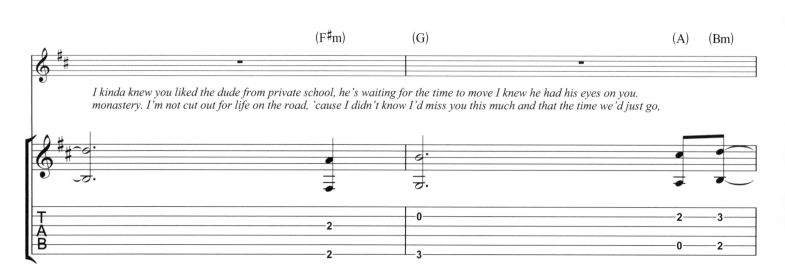

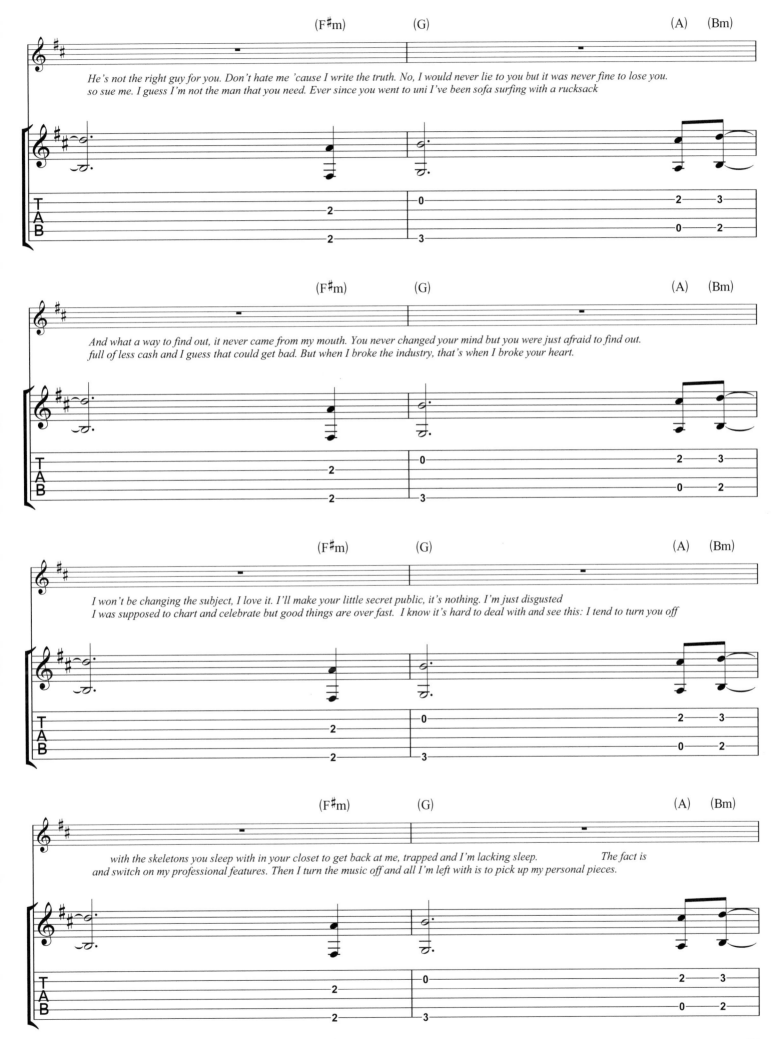

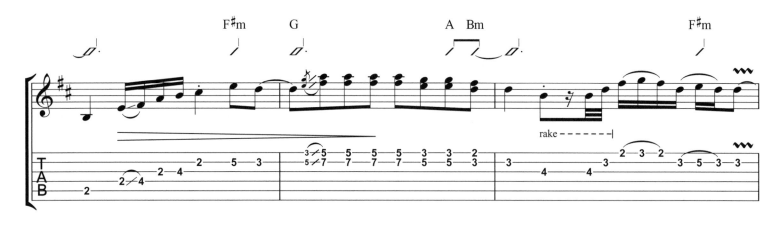

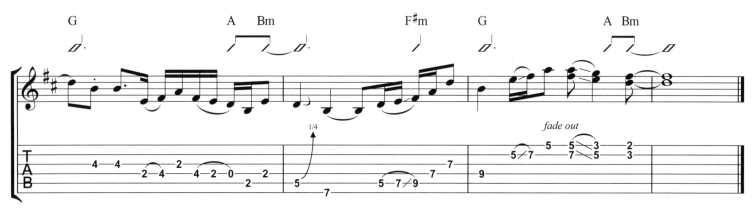

Verse 3:

Since you left I've given up my days off

It's what I need to stay strong

I know you have a day job but mine is 24/7

I feel like writing a book, I guess I lied in the hook

'Cause I still love you and I need you by my side if I could

The irony is if my career and music didn't exist

In six years, yeah, you'd probably be my wife with a kid

I'm frightened to think if I depend on cider and drink

And lighting a spliff, I fall into a spiral and it's just hiding my

Misguiding thoughts that I'm trying to kill

And I'd be writing my will before I'm 27

I'll die from a thrill, go down in history as just a wasted talent

Can I face the challenge or did I make a mistake erasing?

It's only therapy, my thoughts just get ahead of me

Eventually I'll be fine, I know that it was never meant to be

Either way I guess I'm not prepared. But I'll say this:

Things happen for a reason and you can't change

Take my apology. I'm sorry for my honesty, but I had to get this off my chest.

Thinking Out Loud

Words and Music by Ed Sheeran and Amy Wadge

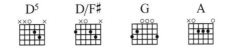

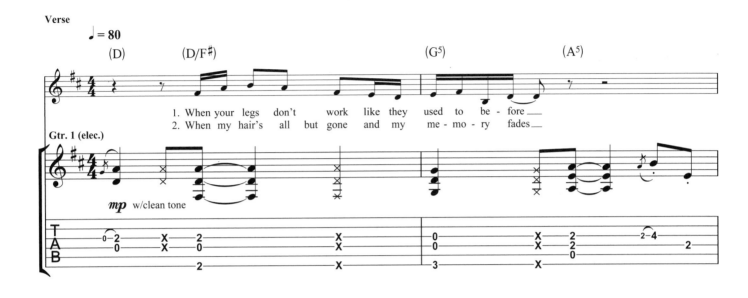

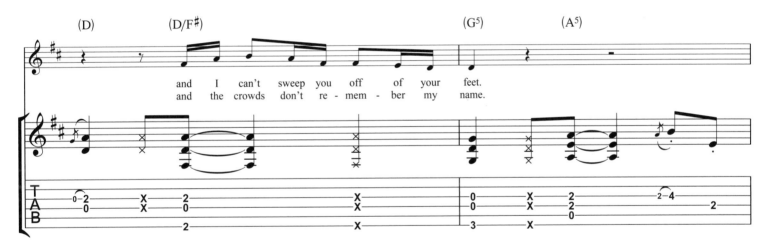

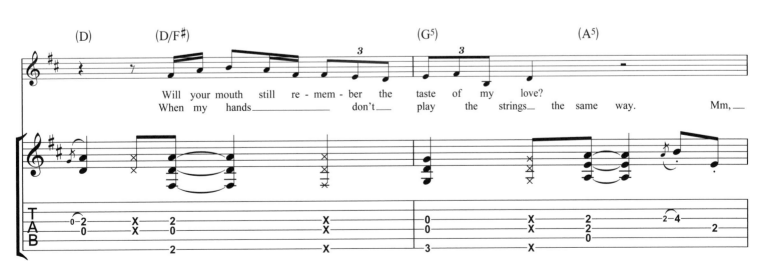

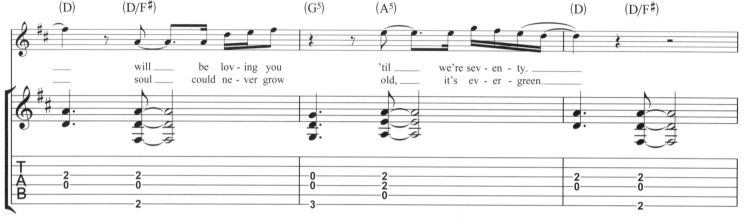

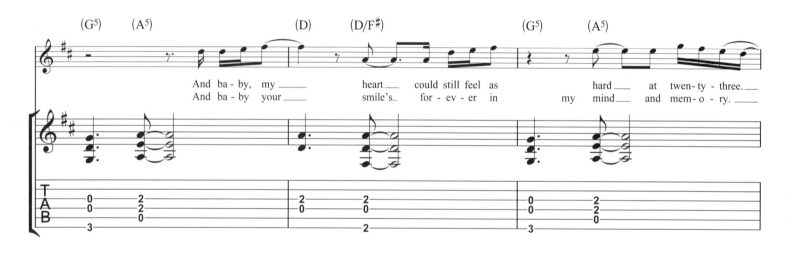

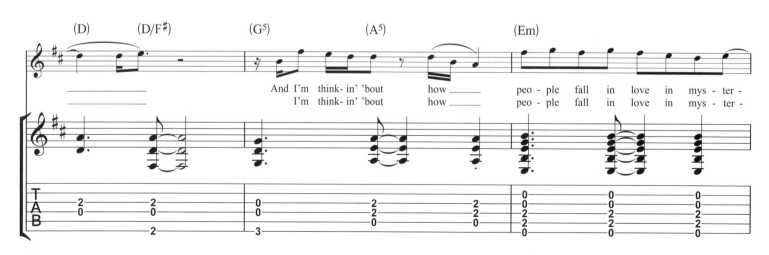

72

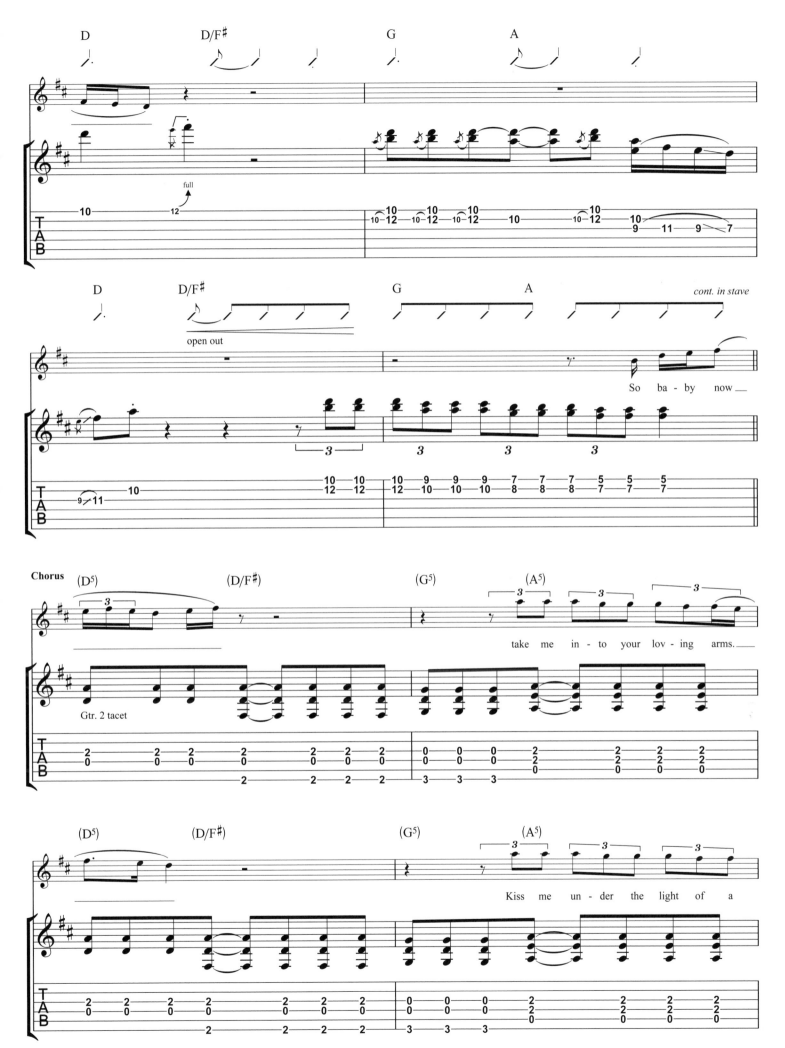

Afire Love

Words and Music by Ed Sheeran, John McDaid, Christophe Beck and Foy Vance

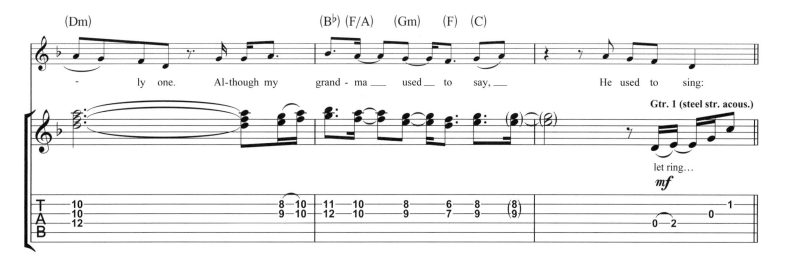

Chorus

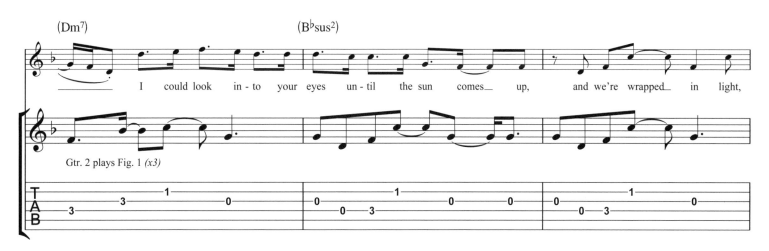

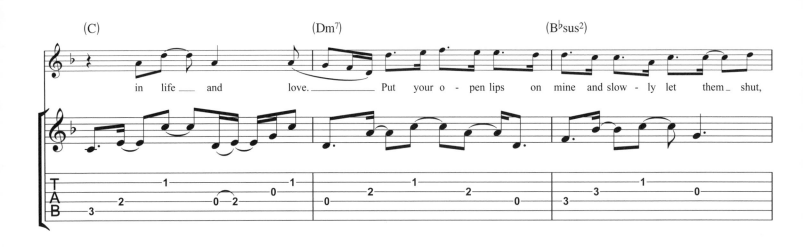

in life ___ and love. ___ Put your o - pen lips on mine and slow - ly let them _ shut,

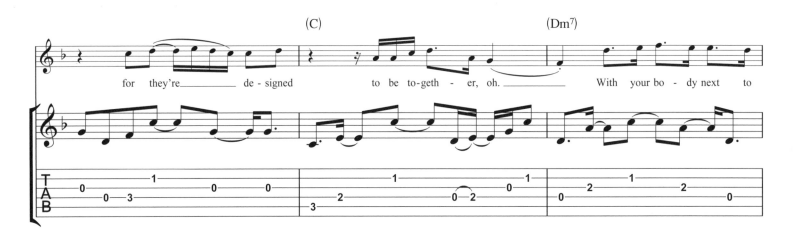

for they're ___ de - signed to be to-geth - er, oh. ___ With your bo - dy next to

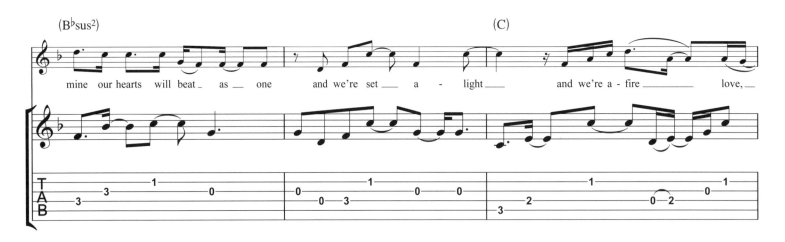

mine our hearts will beat _ as _ one and we're set a - light ___ and we're a - fire ___ love, _

1.

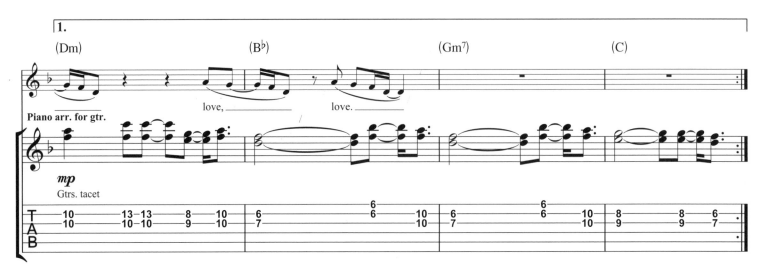

love, ___ love. ___

Piano arr. for gtr.

mp
Gtrs. tacet

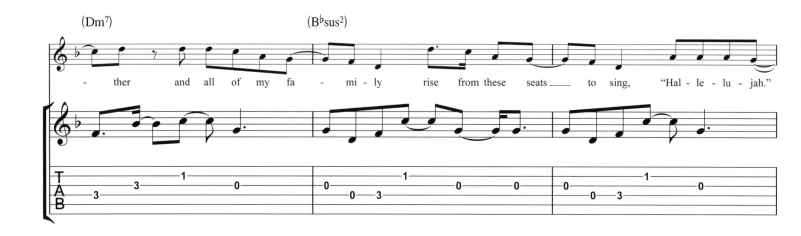

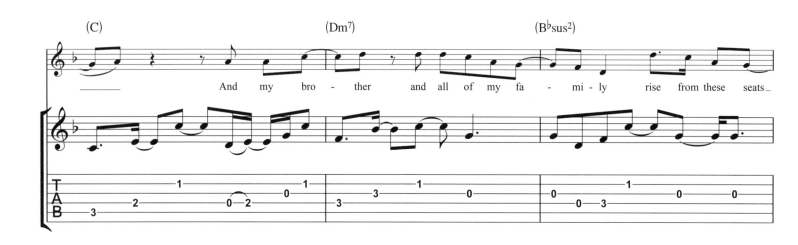

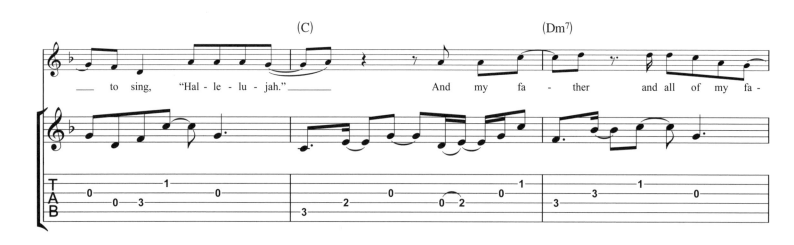

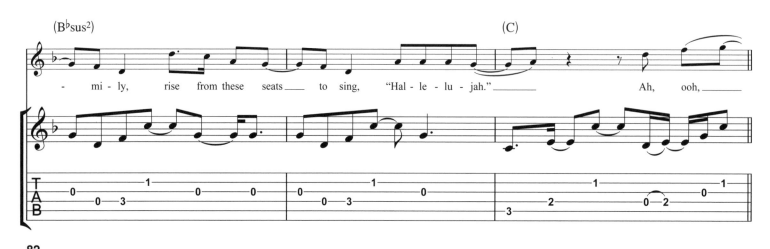

Take It Back

Words and Music by Ed Sheeran and John McDaid

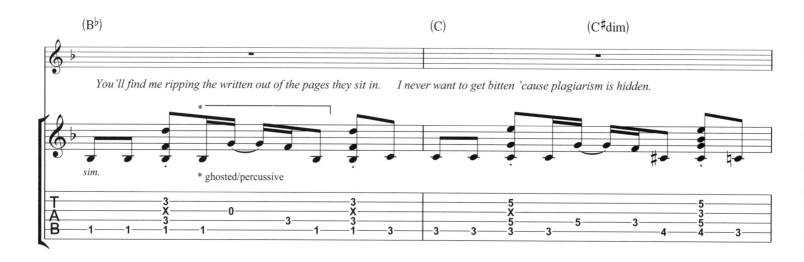

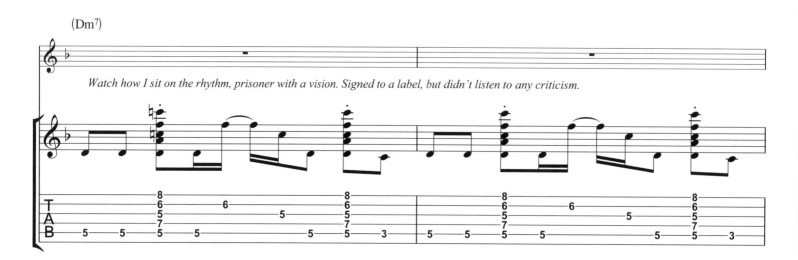

Thought you knew but you didn't, so perk your ears up and listen. Studio is a system and you could say that I'm driven.

And now it's onto the next saga, we drink the best lager. I'll never try to win you over like your stepfather.

I do my own thing now and get respect after, and I'm avoiding the 'caine like it was Get Carter.

For four years I never had a place to stay, but it's safe to say that it kept me grounded like a paperweight.

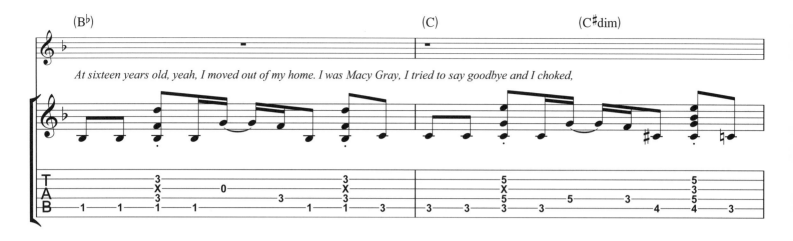

At sixteen years old, yeah, I moved out of my home. I was Macy Gray, I tried to say goodbye and I choked,

and went from sleeping at a subway station to sleeping with a movie star and adding to the population.

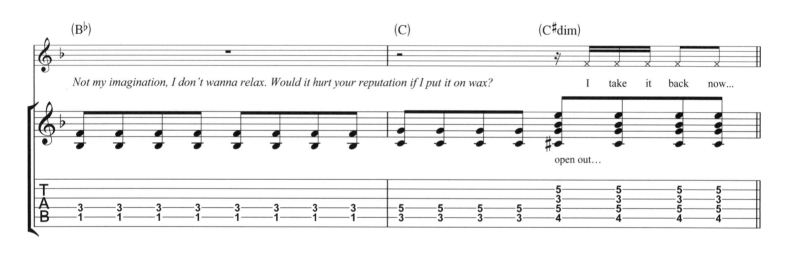

Not my imagination, I don't wanna relax. Would it hurt your reputation if I put it on wax?   I take it back now...

open out...

Chorus

Mm, _____   come on and take it back, love,   come

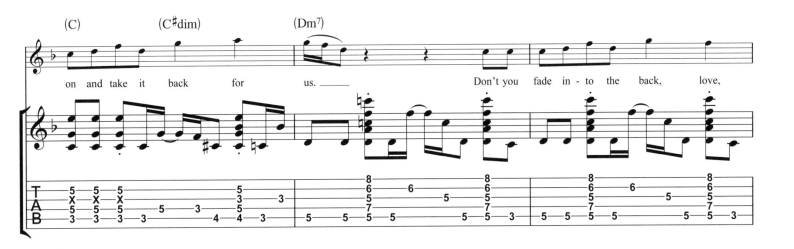

on and take it back for us. ___ Don't you fade in-to the back, love,

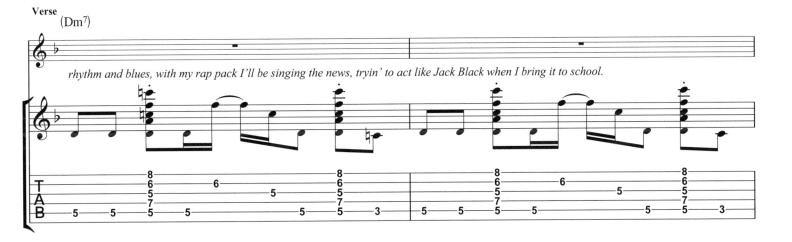

no. ___ 2. I take it back with the

Verse
(Dm⁷)

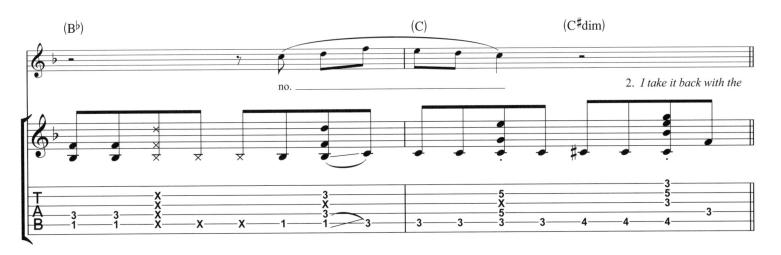

rhythm and blues, with my rap pack I'll be singing the news, tryin' to act like Jack Black when I bring it to school.

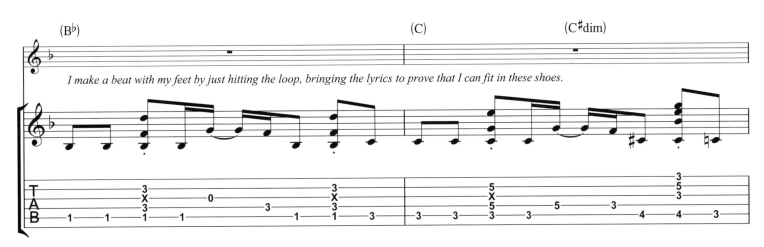

I make a beat with my feet by just hitting the loop, bringing the lyrics to prove that I can fit in these shoes.

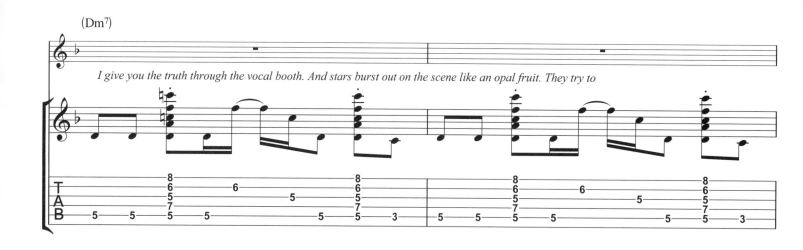

I give you the truth through the vocal booth. And stars burst out on the scene like an opal fruit. They try to

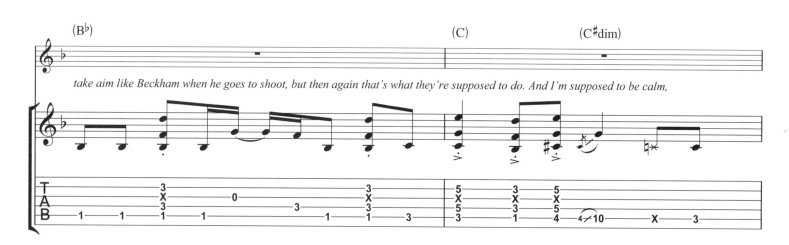

take aim like Beckham when he goes to shoot, but then again that's what they're supposed to do. And I'm supposed to be calm,

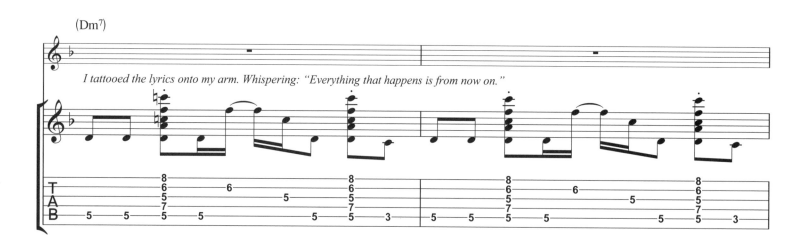

I tattooed the lyrics onto my arm. Whispering: "Everything that happens is from now on."

I'll be ready to start again by the end of the song. Still they're claiming that I handled it wrong. But then I've never had

Chorus

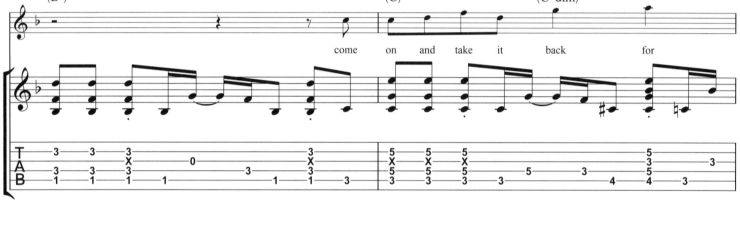

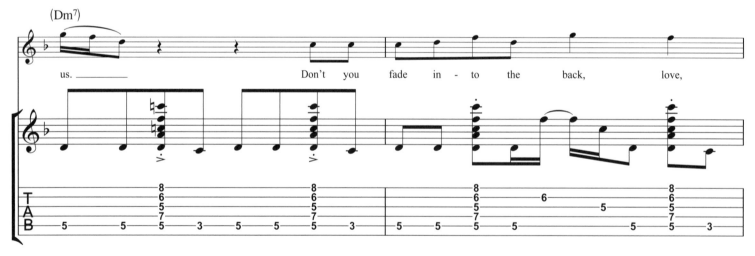

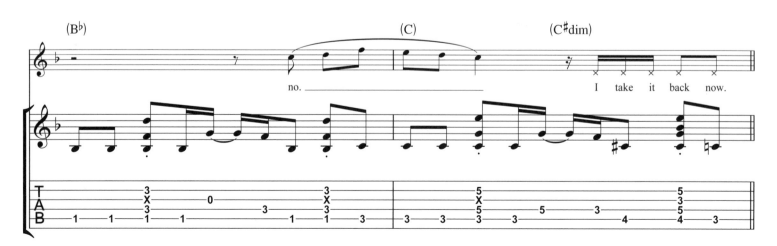

But, but I just write schemes, I'm never having a stylist giving me tight jeans.

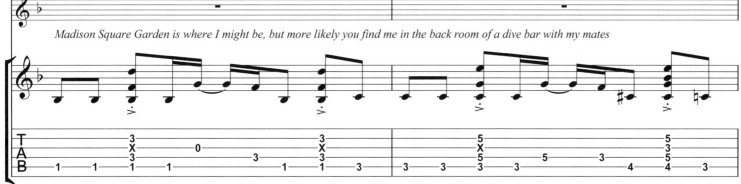

Madison Square Garden is where I might be, but more likely you find me in the back room of a dive bar with my mates

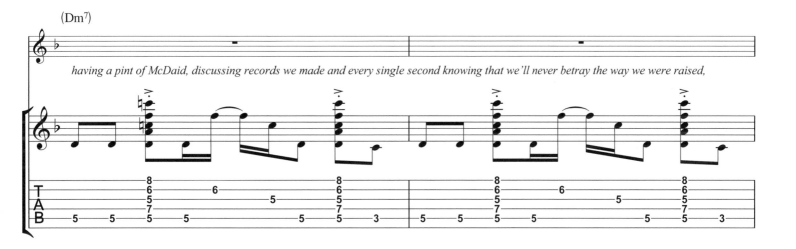

having a pint of McDaid, discussing records we made and every single second knowing that we'll never betray the way we were raised,

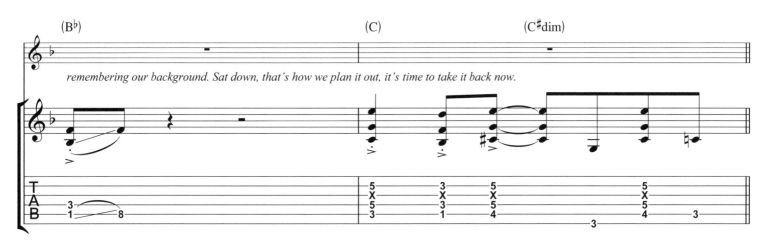

remembering our background. Sat down, that's how we plan it out, it's time to take it back now.

Outro Chorus

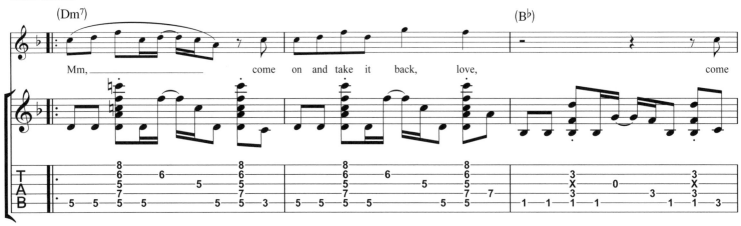

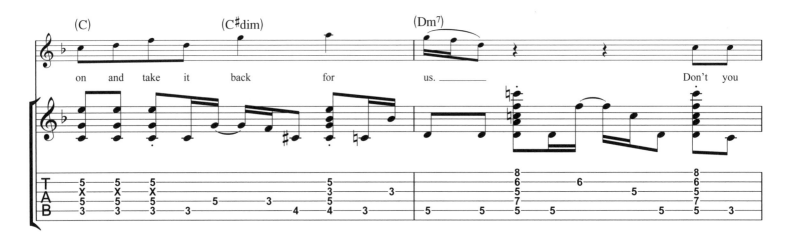

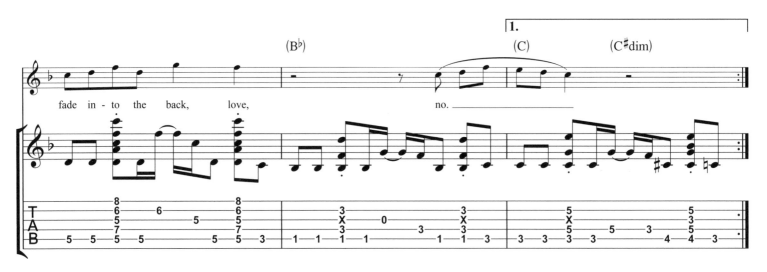

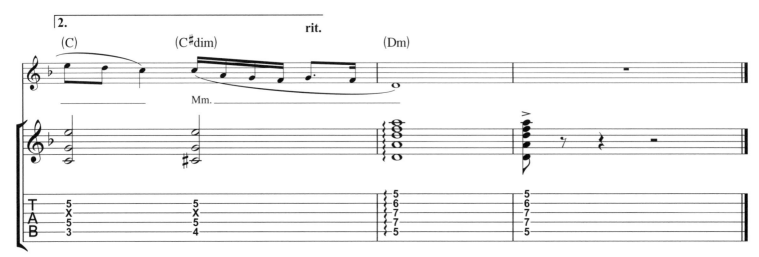

Shirtsleeves

Words and Music by Ed Sheeran

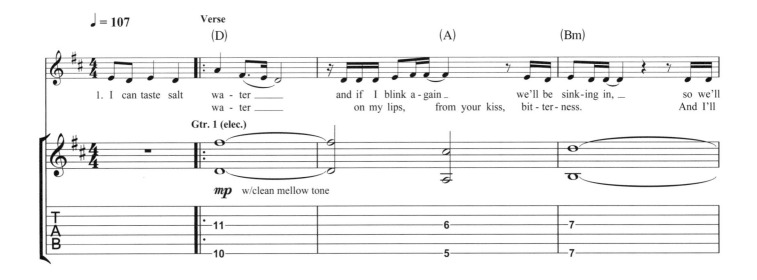

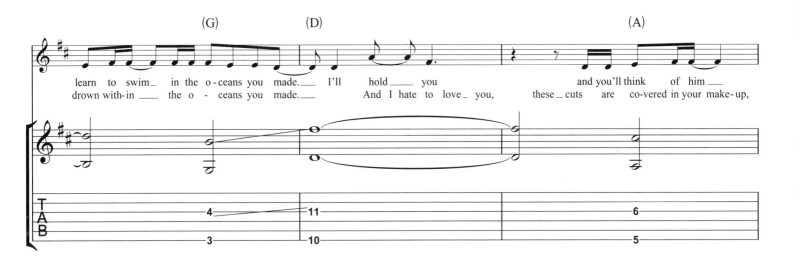

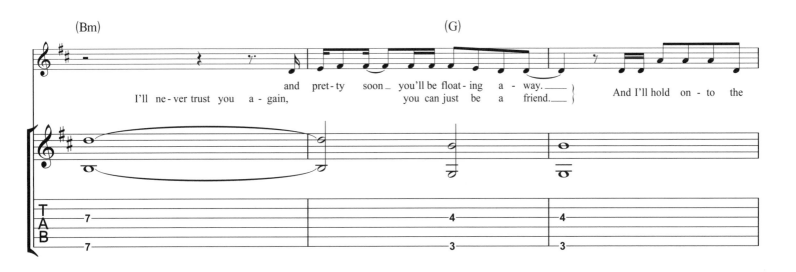

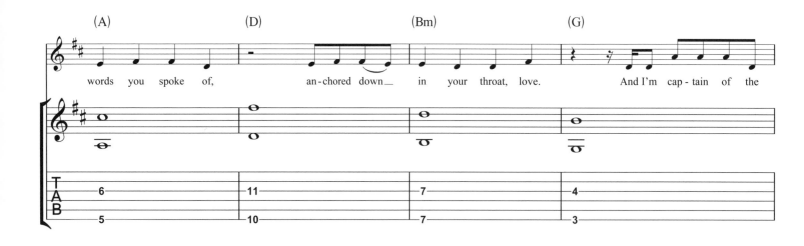

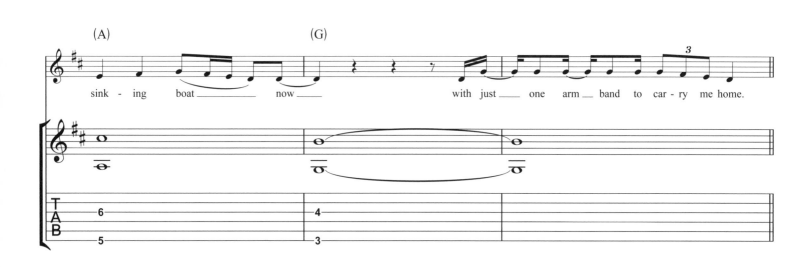

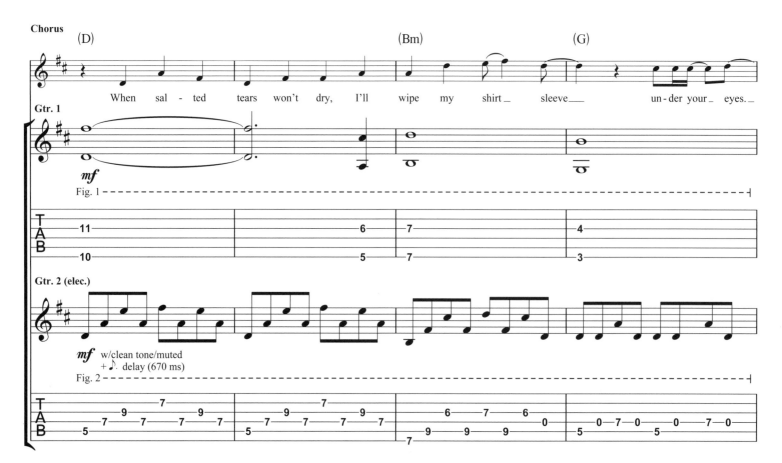

night,   the fact — is I'm,   I'm on the way — home,   I'm on the way — home.

I lied,   I tried   to   cry but I'm, —   I'm drown-ing in — the o - ceans you made.

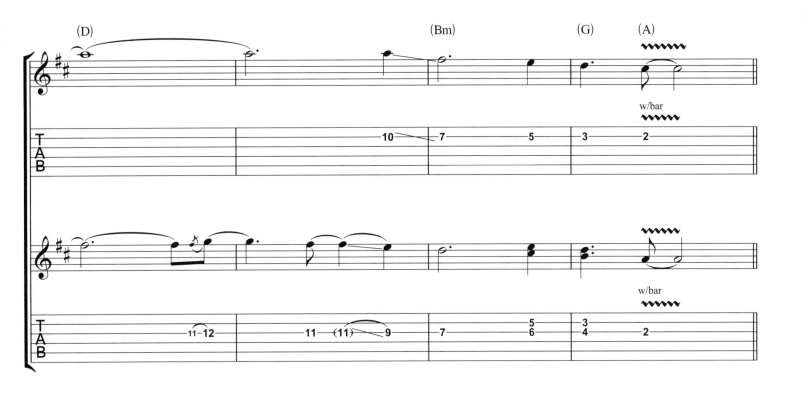

Outro Chorus

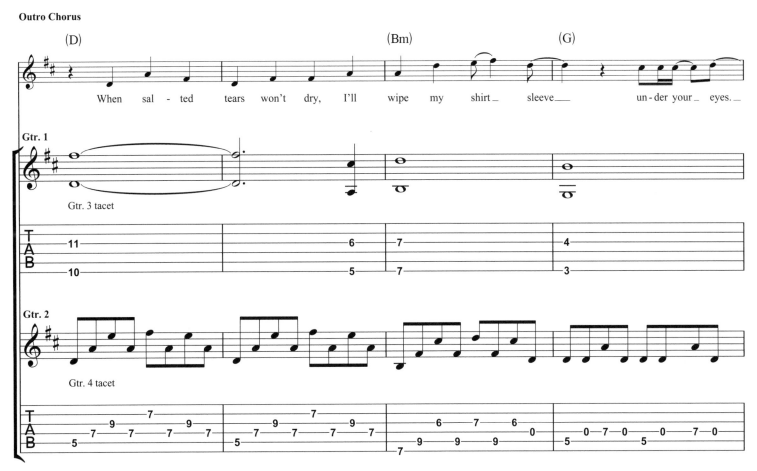

When sal-ted tears won't dry, I'll wipe my shirt sleeve un-der your eyes.

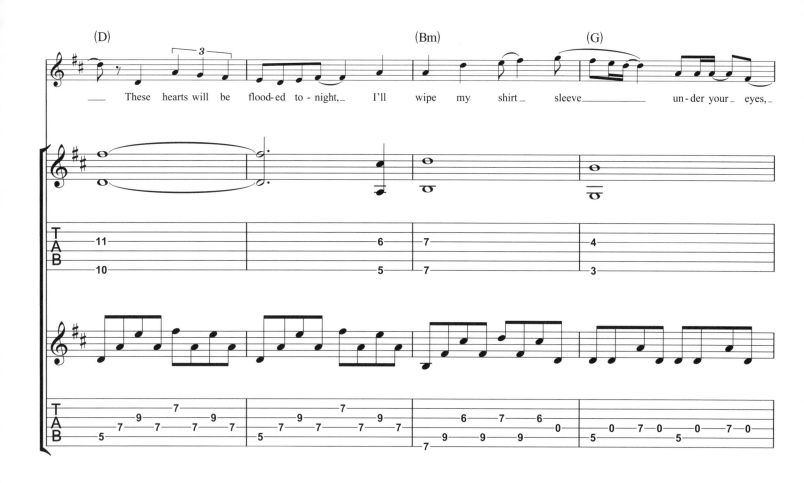

These hearts will be flood-ed to-night,_ I'll wipe my shirt_ sleeve_____ un-der your_ eyes,_

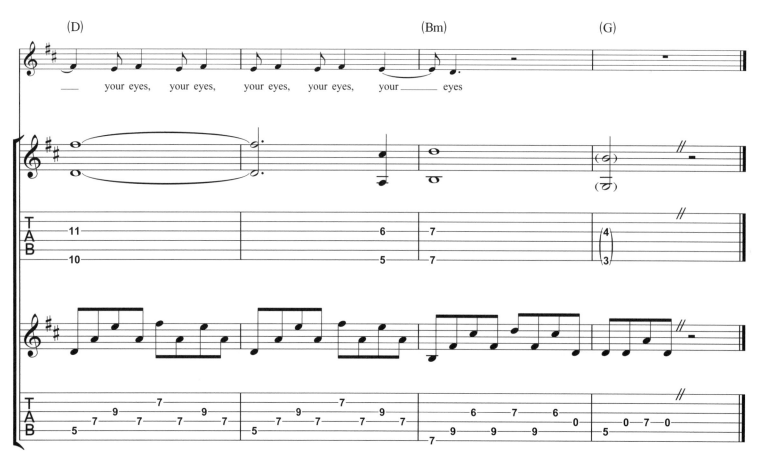

____ your eyes, your eyes, your eyes, your eyes, your _____ eyes

Even My Dad Does Sometimes

Words and Music by Ed Sheeran and Amy Wadge

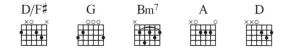

I See Fire

from THE HOBBIT: THE DESOLATION OF SMAUG

Words and Music by Ed Sheeran

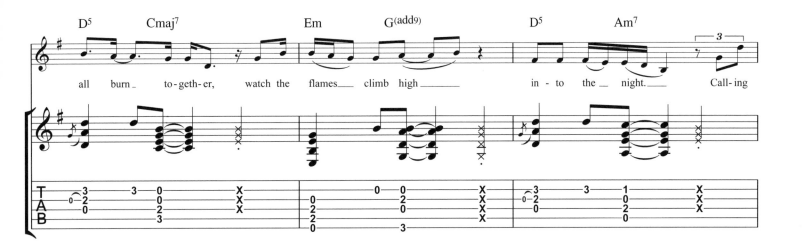

all burn to-geth-er, watch the flames climb high into the night. Call-ing

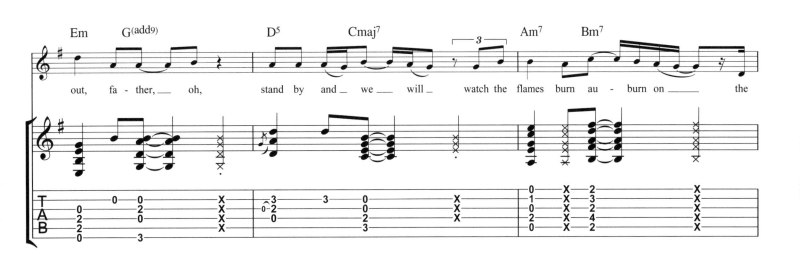

out, fa - ther, oh, stand by and we will watch the flames burn au-burn on the

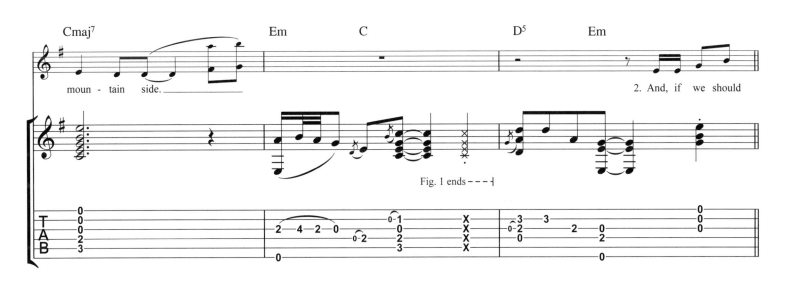

moun - tain side. 2. And, if we should

Fig. 1 ends

Verse

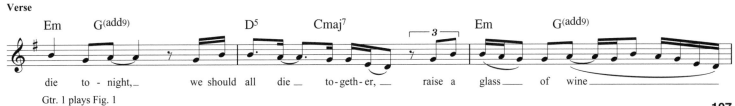

die to - night, we should all die to-geth-er, raise a glass of wine

Gtr. 1 plays Fig. 1

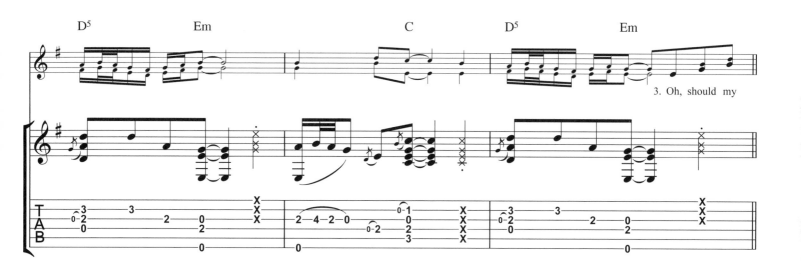

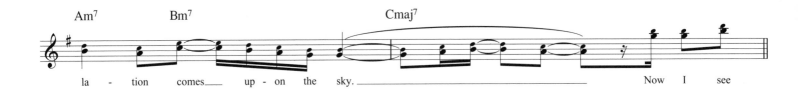

Am⁷   Bm⁷   Cmaj⁷

la - tion comes___ up - on the sky._____ Now I see

Chorus

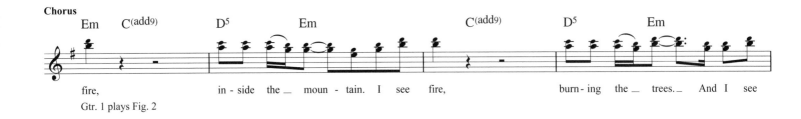

Em   C(add9)   D⁵   Em   C(add9)   D⁵   Em

fire,   in - side the _ moun - tain. I see fire,   burn-ing the _ trees._ And I see

Gtr. 1 plays Fig. 2

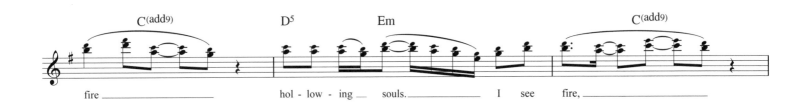

C(add9)   D⁵   Em   C(add9)

fire _____ hol - low - ing _ souls.___ I see fire, _____

D⁵   Am⁷   A⁷(sus4)

Gtr. 1

mp

blood in the _ breeze.___ And I hope that you _ re - mem - ber me. ___ And, if the _

Bridge

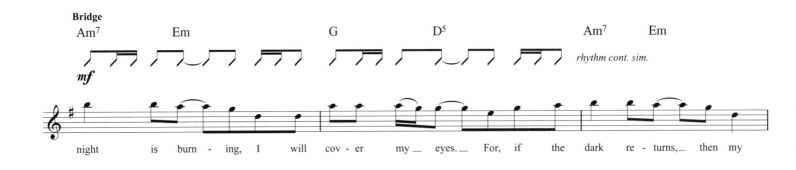

Am⁷   Em   G   D⁵   Am⁷   Em

rhythm cont. sim.

mf

night is burn - ing, I will cov - er my _ eyes._ For, if the dark re - turns,_ then my

G   D⁵   Am⁷   Em   G   D⁵

broth - ers will _ die. And as the sky is fall - ing down,_ it crashed in - to _ this lone - ly town._ And with that

shad-ow up-on the ground, I hear my peo-ple scream-ing out. Now I see

Chorus

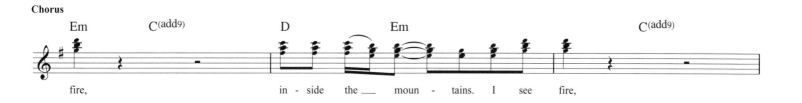

fire, in-side the moun-tains. I see fire,

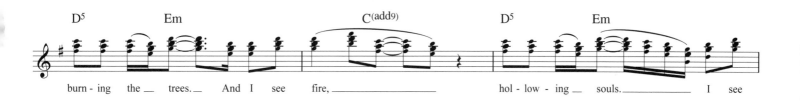

burn-ing the trees. And I see fire, hol-low-ing souls. I see

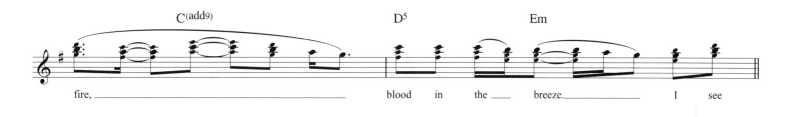

fire, blood in the breeze. I see

Outro

Lead vocal ad lib.

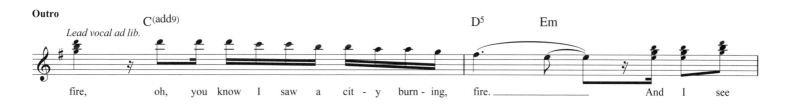

fire, oh, you know I saw a cit-y burn-ing, fire. And I see

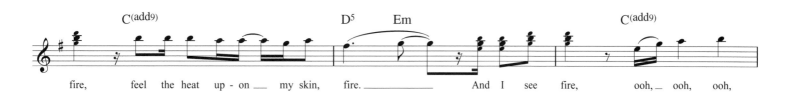

fire, feel the heat up-on my skin, fire. And I see fire, ooh, ooh, ooh,

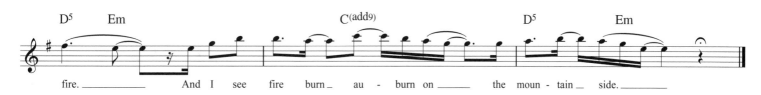

fire. And I see fire burn au-burn on the moun-tain side.

RECORDED VERSIONS®
The Best Note-For-Note Transcriptions Available

AUTHENTIC TRANSCRIPTIONS WITH NOTES AND TABLATURE

14037551	AC/DC – Backtracks	$32.99
00692015	Aerosmith – Greatest Hits	$22.95
00690178	Alice in Chains – Acoustic	$19.95
00694865	Alice in Chains – Dirt	$19.95
00690812	All American Rejects – Move Along	$19.95
00690958	Duane Allman Guitar Anthology	$24.99
00694932	Allman Brothers Band – Volume 1	$24.95
00694933	Allman Brothers Band – Volume 2	$24.95
00694934	Allman Brothers Band – Volume 3	$24.95
00123558	Arctic Monkeys – AM	$22.99
00690609	Audioslave	$19.95
00690820	Avenged Sevenfold – City of Evil	$24.95
00691065	Avenged Sevenfold – Waking the Fallen	$22.99
00690503	Beach Boys – Very Best of	$19.95
00690489	Beatles – 1	$24.99
00694832	Beatles – For Acoustic Guitar	$22.99
00691014	Beatles Rock Band	$34.99
00694914	Beatles – Rubber Soul	$22.99
00694863	Beatles – Sgt. Pepper's Lonely Hearts Club Band	$22.99
00110193	Beatles – Tomorrow Never Knows	$22.99
00690110	Beatles – White Album (Book 1)	$19.95
00691043	Jeff Beck – Wired	$19.99
00692385	Chuck Berry	$19.95
00690835	Billy Talent	$19.95
00690901	Best of Black Sabbath	$19.95
14042759	Black Sabbath – 13	$19.99
00690831	blink-182 – Greatest Hits	$19.95
00690913	Boston	$19.95
00690932	Boston – Don't Look Back	$19.99
00690491	David Bowie – Best of	$19.95
00690873	Breaking Benjamin – Phobia	$19.95
00690451	Jeff Buckley – Collection	$24.95
00690957	Bullet for My Valentine – Scream Aim Fire	$22.99
00691159	The Cars – Complete Greatest Hits	$22.99
00691079	Best of Johnny Cash	$22.99
00690590	Eric Clapton – Anthology	$29.95
00690415	Clapton Chronicles – Best of Eric Clapton	$18.95
00690936	Eric Clapton – Complete Clapton	$29.99
00690074	Eric Clapton – The Cream of Clapton	$24.95
00694869	Eric Clapton – Unplugged	$22.95
00690162	The Clash – Best of	$19.95
00101916	Eric Church – Chief	$22.99
00690828	Coheed & Cambria – Good Apollo I'm Burning Star, IV, Vol. 1: From Fear Through the Eyes of Madness	$19.95
00127184	Best of Robert Cray	$19.99
00690819	Creedence Clearwater Revival – Best of	$22.95
00690648	The Very Best of Jim Croce	$19.95
00690613	Crosby, Stills & Nash – Best of	$22.95
00691171	Cry of Love – Brother	$22.99
00690967	Death Cab for Cutie – Narrow Stairs	$22.99
00690289	Deep Purple – Best of	$19.99
00690784	Def Leppard – Best of	$19.95
00692240	Bo Diddley	$19.99
00122443	Dream Theater	$24.99
14041903	Bob Dylan for Guitar Tab	$19.99
00691186	Evanescence	$22.99
00691181	Five Finger Death Punch – American Capitalist	$22.99
00690664	Fleetwood Mac – Best of	$19.95
00690870	Flyleaf	$19.95
00690808	Foo Fighters – In Your Honor	$19.95
00691115	Foo Fighters – Wasting Light	$22.99
00690805	Robben Ford – Best of	$22.99
00120220	Robben Ford – Guitar Anthology	$24.99

00694920	Free – Best of	$19.95
00691050	Glee Guitar Collection	$19.99
00690943	The Goo Goo Dolls – Greatest Hits Volume 1: The Singles	$22.95
00691190	Best of Peter Green	$19.99
00113073	Green Day – ¡Uno!	$21.99
00116846	Green Day – ¡Dos!	$21.99
00118259	Green Day – ¡Tré!	$21.99
00701764	Guitar Tab White Pages – Play-Along	$39.99
00694854	Buddy Guy – Damn Right, I've Got the Blues	$19.95
00690840	Ben Harper – Both Sides of the Gun	$19.95
00694798	George Harrison – Anthology	$19.95
00690841	Scott Henderson – Blues Guitar Collection	$19.95
00692930	Jimi Hendrix – Are You Experienced?	$24.95
00692931	Jimi Hendrix – Axis: Bold As Love	$22.95
00692932	Jimi Hendrix – Electric Ladyland	$24.95
00690017	Jimi Hendrix – Live at Woodstock	$24.95
00690602	Jimi Hendrix – Smash Hits	$24.99
00119619	Jimi Hendrix – People, Hell and Angels	$22.99
00691152	West Coast Seattle Boy: The Jimi Hendrix Anthology	$29.99
00691332	Jimi Hendrix – Winterland (Highlights)	$22.99
00690793	John Lee Hooker Anthology	$24.99
00690692	Billy Idol – Very Best of	$19.95
00121961	Imagine Dragons – Night Visions	$22.99
00690688	Incubus – A Crow Left of the Murder	$19.95
00690790	Iron Maiden Anthology	$24.99
00690684	Jethro Tull – Aqualung	$19.95
00690814	John5 – Songs for Sanity	$19.95
00690751	John5 – Vertigo	$19.95
00122439	Jack Johnson – From Here to Now to You	$22.99
00690271	Robert Johnson – New Transcriptions	$24.95
00699131	Janis Joplin – Best of	$19.95
00690427	Judas Priest – Best of	$22.99
00120814	Killswitch Engage – Disarm the Descent	$22.99
00124869	Albert King with Stevie Ray Vaughan – In Session	$22.99
00694903	Kiss – Best of	$24.95
00690355	Kiss – Destroyer	$16.95
00690834	Lamb of God – Ashes of the Wake	$19.95
00690875	Lamb of God – Sacrament	$19.95
00690781	Linkin Park – Hybrid Theory	$22.95
00690743	Los Lonely Boys	$19.95
00114563	The Lumineers	$22.99
00690955	Lynyrd Skynyrd – All-Time Greatest Hits	$19.99
00694954	Lynyrd Skynyrd – New Best of	$19.95
00690754	Marilyn Manson – Lest We Forget	$19.95
00694956	Bob Marley – Legend	$19.95
00694945	Bob Marley – Songs of Freedom	$24.95
00690657	Maroon5 – Songs About Jane	$19.95
00120080	Don McLean – Songbook	$19.95
00694951	Megadeth – Rust in Peace	$22.95
00691185	Megadeth – Th1rt3en	$22.99
00690951	Megadeth – United Abominations	$22.99
00690505	John Mellencamp – Guitar Collection	$19.95
00690646	Pat Metheny – One Quiet Night	$19.95
00690558	Pat Metheny – Trio: 99>00	$19.95
00118836	Pat Metheny – Unity Band	$22.99
00690040	Steve Miller Band – Young Hearts	$19.95
00119338	Ministry Guitar Tab Collection	$24.99
00102591	Wes Montgomery Guitar Anthology	$24.99
00691070	Mumford & Sons – Sigh No More	$22.99
00694883	Nirvana – Nevermind	$19.95
00690026	Nirvana – Unplugged in New York	$19.95
00690807	The Offspring – Greatest Hits	$19.95
00694847	Ozzy Osbourne – Best of	$22.95
00690399	Ozzy Osbourne – Ozzman Cometh	$22.99
00690933	Best of Brad Paisley	$22.95
00690995	Brad Paisley – Play: The Guitar Album	$24.99
00694855	Pearl Jam – Ten	$22.99
00690439	A Perfect Circle – Mer De Noms	$19.95
00690499	Tom Petty – Definitive Guitar Collection	$19.95
00121933	Pink Floyd – Acoustic Guitar Collection	$22.99
00690428	Pink Floyd – Dark Side of the Moon	$19.95

00690789	Poison – Best of	$19.95
00694975	Queen – Greatest Hits	$24.95
00690670	Queensryche – Very Best of	$19.95
00109303	Radiohead Guitar Anthology	$24.99
00694910	Rage Against the Machine	$19.95
00119834	Rage Against the Machine – Guitar Anthology	$22.99
00690055	Red Hot Chili Peppers – Blood Sugar Sex Magik	$19.95
00690584	Red Hot Chili Peppers – By the Way	$19.95
00691166	Red Hot Chili Peppers – I'm with You	$22.99
00690852	Red Hot Chili Peppers –Stadium Arcadium	$24.95
00690511	Django Reinhardt – Definitive Collection	$19.95
00690779	Relient K – MMHMM	$19.95
00690631	Rolling Stones – Guitar Anthology	$27.95
00694976	Rolling Stones – Some Girls	$22.95
00690264	The Rolling Stones – Tattoo You	$19.95
00690685	David Lee Roth – Eat 'Em and Smile	$19.95
00690942	David Lee Roth and the Songs of Van Halen	$19.95
00690031	Santana's Greatest Hits	$19.95
00690566	Scorpions – Best of	$22.95
00690604	Bob Seger – Guitar Collection	$19.95
00690803	Kenny Wayne Shepherd Band – Best of	$19.95
00690968	Shinedown – The Sound of Madness	$22.99
00122218	Skillet – Rise	$22.99
00691114	Slash – Guitar Anthology	$24.99
00690813	Slayer – Guitar Collection	$19.95
00120004	Steely Dan – Best of	$24.95
00694921	Steppenwolf – Best of	$22.95
00690655	Mike Stern – Best of	$19.95
00690877	Stone Sour – Come What(ever) May	$19.95
00690520	Styx Guitar Collection	$19.95
00120081	Sublime	$19.95
00120122	Sublime – 40oz. to Freedom	$19.95
00690929	Sum 41 – Underclass Hero	$19.95
00690767	Switchfoot – The Beautiful Letdown	$19.95
00690993	Taylor Swift – Fearless	$22.99
00115957	Taylor Swift – Red	$21.99
00690531	System of a Down – Toxicity	$19.95
00694824	James Taylor – Best of	$17.99
00690871	Three Days Grace – One-X	$19.95
00123862	Trivium – Vengeance Falls	$22.99
00690683	Robin Trower – Bridge of Sighs	$19.95
00660137	Steve Vai – Passion & Warfare	$24.95
00110385	Steve Vai – The Story of Light	$22.99
00690116	Stevie Ray Vaughan – Guitar Collection	$24.95
00660058	Stevie Ray Vaughan – Lightnin' Blues 1983-1987	$24.95
00694835	Stevie Ray Vaughan – The Sky Is Crying	$22.95
00690015	Stevie Ray Vaughan – Texas Flood	$19.95
00690772	Velvet Revolver – Contraband	$22.95
00690071	Weezer (The Blue Album)	$19.95
00690966	Weezer – (Red Album)	$19.99
00691941	The Who – Acoustic Guitar Collection	$22.99
00690447	The Who – Best of	$24.95
00122303	Yes Guitar Collection	$22.99
00690916	The Best of Dwight Yoakam	$19.95
00691020	Neil Young – After the Gold Rush	$22.99
00691019	Neil Young – Everybody Knows This Is Nowhere	$19.99
00691021	Neil Young – Harvest Moon	$22.99
00690905	Neil Young – Rust Never Sleeps	$19.99
00690623	Frank Zappa – Over-Nite Sensation	$22.99
00121684	ZZ Top – Early Classics	$24.99
00690589	ZZ Top Guitar Anthology	$24.95

COMPLETE SERIES LIST ONLINE!

HAL•LEONARD® CORPORATION
7777 W. BLUEMOUND RD. P.O. BOX 13819 MILWAUKEE, WI 53213

www.halleonard.com

Prices and availability subject to change without notice.
Some products may not be available outside the U.S.A.

0714